T0353106

Murder & Crime

MEDWAY

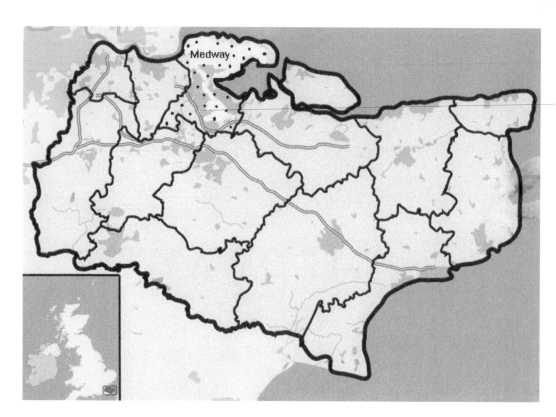

Medway

GATEWAY, HIGH STREET, ROCHESTER

Murder& Crime

MEDWAY

JANET CAMERON

ACKNOWLEDGEMENTS

With special thanks for kind permission to use photographs: Stephen Rayner, *Medway News*, Marc Demarest and Richard Platt. Also to my editors, Nicola Guy, Claire Forbes and Simon Holt for all their encouragement and support, Rene Wallace for sharing her good ideas, Brian Mulvaney for helpful suggestions.

Frontispiece:
Left: Map of Kent showing Medway's boundaries.
Right: The Gateway, High Street, Rochester.

Inside front cover:
After Caesar first landed in England in 55 BC, he described the men of Kent (or Cantium) as the 'most civilised.' I shall leave you to be the judge of this after you have finished reading the book!

First published in 2008

Reprinted 2011, 2012

The History Press
The Mill, Brimscombe Port,
Stroud, Gloucestershire, GL5 2QG
www.thehistorypress.co.uk

© Janet Cameron, 2008

The right of Janet Cameron to be identified as the Author
of this work has been asserted in accordance with the
Copyrights, Designs and Patents Act 1988.

All rights reserved. No part of this book may be reprinted
or reproduced or utilised in any form or by any electronic,
mechanical or other means, now known or hereafter invented,
including photocopying and recording, or in any information
storage or retrieval system, without the permission in writing
from the Publishers.

British Library Cataloguing in Publication Data.
A catalogue record for this book is available from the British Library.

ISBN 978 0 7524 4541 0

Typesetting and origination by
The History Press
Printed in Great Britain

SOME IMPORTANT PLACE NAMES

ORIGINS: ROCHESTER, CHAHAM, STROOD, GILLINGHAM AND RAINHAM

Kent: The county's name is derived from *cantus*, which means border. In 51 BC, Caesar called Kent *Cantium;* later it became *Cantia*. Kent's earliest people were called *Cantwara* and their capital was *Canterbury*.

THE MEDWAY TOWNS

Rochester: This name is derived from the Latin word *castra*, which is present in cities dating from Roman times.

Gillingham: (*ham* = homestead, *ingas* = family. Hence, homestead of Gylla's family. In the tenth century, it was known as Gyllingeham and, in some old texts, as Jillingham Water. In the Domesday book in 1086, it is mentioned as Gelingeham. Gillingham was a small fishing village which developed around the area of St Mary's Church, dedicated to St Mary Magdelene. In the Middle Ages, the story of 'Our Lady of Gillingham', who worked miracles, was exploited by locals for the benefit of pilgrims on their way to the tomb of St Thomas Beckett in Canterbury. Another theory is that the name may be derived from the old English *gylian* or *gyllan*, meaning to shout – thus, the shouting men.

Strood: '*Strod*' or '*strop*' means marshy land overgrown with brushwood, a similar meaning to Stroud in Gloucestershire.

Chatham: Forest settlement. In 1184, Chatham was known as Chatteham.

Rainham: Settlement (*ham*) of the ruling, or powerful, men, the Rœgingas. In a charter of 811, Rainham was described as a royal town.

OTHER IMPORTANT MEDWAY PLACE NAMES

Borstal: a place of safety.

Twydall: (an area of Gillingham) Meaning 'double portion' or 'dole' from the old English 'twidael'. (From 1240-1690 variations of Twydele, Twydole, Twidall)

Upchurch: As you would expect, this means a church standing high up. The church spire was once used by seamen as a landmark.

Upnor: This means upon the bank, due to a building predating Upnor Castle, recorded at Upnore in 1374.

Wigmore: Wide pool, (Wydemere, 1275) from Old English.

Above: Rochester Bridge in 1828. (Courtesy of Stephen Rayner and *Medway News*)

Below: Rochester Bridge in 2007.

Coat of Arms on Rochester Bridge. The bridge is toll-free and that is the meaning of *publica privatis* – from the private for the public.

The Police Band marching along Rochester High Street, Dickens Festival, 2007.

Gillingham's main shopping centre, 2007.

CONTENTS

The River Medway.

INTRODUCTION

Crimes of violence and cruelty offend human nature regardless of when or where they take place. But sometimes a lack of perception or understanding due to ignorance might cause people to act cruelly or immorally. Examples might be the practice of circuses using performing animals or of corporal punishment. There are also crimes considered to be immoral during earlier periods of history which might be regarded as normal behaviour today.

'I can't understand it. He was always such a nice man. To think he could ever have committed such a terrible crime!' How many times have you heard those words during news reports on the television, generally spoken by the neighbours or workmates of a violent criminal?

The psychology of murder is not specific. Psychological disorders that lead to a human being taking terrible revenge on another human being do not have precise definitions. Human nature can be so complex as to make it impossible to guess that a certain harmless-looking neighbour might be capable of such a terrible crime. That's the most terrifying aspect of the most successful criminals, their apparent *ordinariness*.

People point out, 'It's the quiet ones who should be watched.' This is because it's the quiet ones who may be holding everything inside, all those bitter feelings fermenting, intensifying, preparing to explode. Those who get openly angry can sometimes get it all out of their systems. But not always, because there are no absolutes. And that is what makes the contemplation of murder so fascinating.

THE MEDWAY TOWNS –
AN OVERVIEW

The three tribes which conquered Britain, the Angles, Saxons and Jutes, began their occupation around AD 450. The Jutes settled in Kent. Their colonisation was challenged periodically by the aggressive Danes who managed to penetrate via the Medway and who succeeded in sacking Rochester in AD 842. There must be something especially robust about Kentish resistance since the invaders never managed to infiltrate Kent as thoroughly as they did the Midlands and the North of England.

THE NORMAN INVASION

After the Norman Invasion of 1066, William I gave Kent to his obnoxious half-brother Odo, Bishop of Bayeux, who caused no end of trouble for everyone at a time when ordinary lives were controlled by the church and a hierarchical feudal system. Common people laboured on farms, for their subsistence and for the profit of their masters, while the King, at the top of the tree, owned all the land, which he could dispose of as he chose. Corruption was rife, for rich landowners offered the King money to avoid military service.

The River Medway lies between the Isle of Grain and the Kent mainland and it was here the Normans erected two of the area's most distinctive landmarks; beautiful Rochester Castle whose magnificent square keep dominates the skyline above the river, and Rochester Cathedral with its exquisite architecture.

War was a fact of life and the original stone Rochester Bridge, built in 1387, was erected as a result of profits from the Hundred Years War with France and replaced a wooden Saxon bridge from 960. (Two more bridges succeeded the 1387 version. An iron bridge was built in 1856 and the present bridge was erected in 1914).

REVOLT AGAINST REPRESSION

Apart from foreign wars, there were also, of course, a number of 'civil' wars. Medway had more than its fair share of heroes over the years. Wat Tyler's Rebellion in 1381, known as The Peasants' Revolt, was a stand against oppression. Although Tyler came from nearby Maidstone, there were many feisty Medway stalwarts counted among his supporters. Two of them were Thomas Berghestede and Robert Prat, both from Gillingham, who extracted charters and documents from a certain Thomas Bedemanton on 9 June 1381. No doubt they felt they were entirely justified. Later, in 1450, Jack Cade stood against the excesses of taxation by leading a march of Kentish and Sussex men to London. In 1554, there was another Kent hero, Sir Thomas Wyatt, the son of a poet, who opposed Mary's marriage to Philip II of Spain and, likewise, probably recruited Medway support when he marched in protest from Allingham Castle.

Five Medway views on an old postcard.

Above left: Rochester Cathedral.

Above right: Old Rochester Castle, scene of many a battle.

Restoration House, above, was used in the film 'Great Expectations' to represent Charles Dickens' Satis House.

MEDDLESOME HENRY TUDOR

Tudor times presented Medway with other new challenges. Rochester's Priory of St Andrews became a victim of Henry VIII's dissolution of the monasteries and the confiscation of their treasure. This was later replaced in 1541 with a new chapter and The King's School was built where the original ancient college had been attached to the priory. Medway was also the stage for a major historic event when, in December, 1540, King Henry VIII met his future bride, Anne of Cleaves. Anne was watching a bull-baiting in the King's Palace located in the old priory buildings and did not expect to be secretly observed, nor was she prepared for what Henry actually looked like. Unannounced, Henry walked in on Anne and took a violent dislike to her, although this may have been due to her reaction to him. Henry begged Cromwell to find him a legal way out of the marriage, but England couldn't risk offending the Germans. Henry and Anne were married at Greenwich on 6 January 1540.

Later, in 1573, Elizabeth I, daughter of Henry VIII, came to admire her fleet anchored in the River Medway. She dined in Rochester with the city's MP, Richard Watts, at Boley Hill. As she was leaving, Richard asked her if her visit had been to her liking and she replied '*satis*' which is Latin for 'enough'. Her approving comment provided the house with a name – Satis House.

The River Medway became a centre for shipbuilding and kept the Royal Navy supplied with vessels. In 1547, Chatham Dockyard was established. In 1581, 400ft of wharfage appeared. As time passed into the seventeenth century, ships were increasing in size and had difficulty navigating the River Medway. Eventually, sandbanks prevented large vessel access to the dockyard at certain times. Chatham Dockyard was extended during the nineteenth century. This project cost £3 million and took over thirty years to complete. There were also private yards for shipbuilding during Elizabeth I's reign. The *Mayflower*, famous ship of the Pilgrim Fathers, was launched at Strood.

THE DICKENS' CONNECTION

Medway's unique and colourful history, both military and literary, has fascinating connections with Dickens' times. Chertsey's Gate, a feature of the old monastery precinct, was used by Charles Dickens for his novel *The Mystery of Edwin Drood* and John Jasper's home. *Pickwick Papers* and *Great Expectations* both mention the Royal Victoria and Bull Hotel, an eighteenth-century coaching inn.

GILLINGHAM'S WARRIOR HERO

Will Adams was an explorer and the first Englishman to go to Japan, where the Japanese Shogun made him a samurai. A roundabout and a road are named after him.

THE GOOD, THE BAD AND THE TERRIBLE

Rochester and Chatham have always been vibrant, active towns, just as they are today, attracting wealth and privilege with their military importance and fine street markets which brought in people from the neighbouring area. Education became more widespread and, as a result, law and medicine became a part of life. Rochester's Guildhall was built in 1687 and the Corn Exchange appeared in 1698, although originally it was the Butcher's Market. Its intricate facade was added in 1706. Skilled workers gradually formed guilds to ensure their own protection.

THE HAVES AND THE HAVE-NOTS

When seamen began to explore the world, bringing back exotic goods like spices and tobacco, the nation became wealthier and more powerful. However, a great divide occurred between the 'haves' and the 'have-nots'. After Henry VIII's dissolution of the monasteries, destitute people no longer had anyone to care for them, since this important duty been undertaken by the monks. The numbers of poor and desperate people increased rapidly, forcing legislation.

The sixteenth-century Poor Law made the care of the unemployed, disabled and infirm the responsibility of the parish. In 1576 a statute was added that the able-bodied poor should be required to work and, by the latter part of the eighteenth century, the wages of low-paid workers were supplemented by a parish allowance. In 1834, this system was abandoned. The so-called 'deserving poor' gained relief through the workhouses, while the 'undeserving poor' were sent to houses of correction, an even harsher regime than the workhouses.

As the eighteenth century tipped over into the nineteenth, great changes were afoot. Revolutions in France and America affected Kent as they did other parts of the British Isles. This

Above: Chatham Dockyard, main gate.

Left: The Richmond Road Navy Army & Air Force Institute provided a bolthole for ordinary men as it was not acceptable for commissioned officers to interfere with their relaxation. The site is now occupied by a welding company.

Opposite above: Road sign approaching historic Chatham and the Medway Tunnel.

Opposite below: Medway's fine modern police station near the university campus.

situation was exacerbated by the Poor Law and inflation. Working men were poorer in 1815 than they had been in the mid-1790s. Mob violence and criminal activity stretched the police force to its limit. According to the 1801 census, which was the first official census, the population of Kent amounted to 300,000, most of whom were employed on the land. Fortunately, by the early twentieth century, a system of social security replaced the repressive Poor Law.

THE DEFENCE OF THE MEDWAY TOWNS

Medway's forts were first built to defend the Dockyard against Napoleonic forces and comprised two circles. During the Napoleonic Wars a series of forts forming an inner circle were built. These were Forts Pitt, Clarence, Amherst and Gillingham. Around 1860 an outer circle of forts comprised Forts Borstal, Bridgewood, Luton and Twydall Redoubts; also two forts on an island in the Medway, Forts Hoo and Darnet. All have interesting histories; for example, after 1815 Fort Clarence became both a prison and then a lunatic asylum. Flogging in the prison made sensational copy for the local papers. Fort Clarence's brick gun tower still remains and there is also a section of ditch which runs from St Margaret's Street into gardens opposite. The tower has now been converted into apartments.

A POPULATION EXPLOSION

Due to the expansion of the dockyard, and the barracks for the soldiers at Brompton, the population of Chatham increased from 5,000 at the beginning of the eighteenth century to over 10,000 in 1801. By 1901, the figures had mushroomed to 37,000, a phenomenal rate of growth. The Historical Dockyard now covers the 80 acres which were formerly occupied by the Royal Navy Chatham Dockyard and which closed in 1984.

Twenty-first century Medway has seen several major developments, for example the widening of the A2/M2 motorways between Cobham and Junction 4, involving the excavation of 7 million cu. m of earth. This project was combined with the construction of the new 1km Medway Bridge running 30m over the river and located between the existing Medway Bridge and the Channel Tunnel Rail Link Bridge. The improved links created across the south-east and Europe should help to promote new employment and opportunities for the people of Medway.

I

EARLY CRIME IN THE MEDWAY AREA

A fair trial hasn't always been valued as it is today. The tenth-century King Athelsten made the following pronouncement: 'that if a thief fled he should be pursued to his death by all men ... and whosoever shall meet him shall kill him.' In those dark days, if property or vengeance was desired, then it was up to the aggrieved party to take action, possibly with the help of his family or friends. This is where the term 'hue and cry' came from – it was up to a citizen to raise the alarm if he witnessed a crime – if he failed, then he himself could be punished. Around the thirteenth century, high constables were appointed and later petty constables were employed to assist him in ensuring law and order. (At least, after a fashion; there were many complaints about the constables' inefficiency.)

A POOR REWARD FOR GOODNESS

Described either as William of Perth or William of Rochester, this patron saint of adopted children was born in Perth in the twelfth century and died at Rochester after having his throat cut in 1201. William was, allegedly, a bad lot during his early years but in young adulthood he converted to Christianity, committing himself to God, attending mass daily and caring for unfortunate and neglected children. Working as a baker, he gave every tenth loaf to the poor. One day, while walking to church, he found a small abandoned child on a threshold and decided to adopt him and instruct him in the art of baking. William named the child David.

Many years later, on a pilgrimage to the Holy Land, William and David fell out just as they reached Rochester. Unexpectedly, David turned on his rescuer, clubbed him, slit his throat and then robbed him, before fleeing for his life. A passing woman, who happened to suffer from madness, discovered the body and made a necklace of honeysuckle flowers which she placed on it. Then she put the garland on herself and a miracle happened – her insanity was lifted from her. This impressed some monks, who decided William's final resting place should be within the cathedral. A shrine in the form of a tomb and chapel became a focus for pilgrims and its remains can still be seen near St William's Hospital, although unfortunately, his relics were destroyed with the cathedral in 1538 during Henry VIII's reign of terror. William was canonised in 1256 by Pope Innocent IV, at the suggestion of the Bishop of Rochester, Lawrence de San Martino.

A POT FULL OF FIRE

A report in the *London Eyre* of 1244 cites a maidservant, Inga, instructed by her mistress, together with a Norman, Roger le Sauser, to travel to Gore Farm, Upchurch with a 'pot full of fire', to destroy the manor house. Roger le Sauser killed the occupant with an arrow and set fire to the house, burning it down. Fleeing to the church at Upchurch, Roger promised to 'abjure the Realm' and leave England forever for Normandy, and so managed to escape. Inga, obliged to return to her mistress, was less fortunate and was tried and convicted of arson and murder; then burned at the stake, simply for following her mistress' orders.

MISTAKEN IDENTITY

On Good Friday in the year 1264, Simon de Montfort, (the one who led the barons in opposition to of King Henry III of England) attacked Rochester Castle. But de Montfort was repelled by Ralph de Capo's spirited resistance. Ralph probably had good reason to fight so valiantly for the castle because it contained his future bride, the beautiful Lady Blanche de Warenne. As his enemies began to retreat, Ralph was still spoiling for a fight and left the castle in pursuit of the upstarts.

One of the attacking soldiers was Gilbert de Clare, who had a soft spot for Lady Blanche although she'd rejected him in favour of Ralph – a preference Gilbert found hard to accept or even understand. Amidst the chaos, and seeing that Ralph had disappeared, Gilbert de Clare decided it might be worth trying again to convince Blanche of his suitability to be her lover. Sneaking into the castle, he soon located Lady Blanche on the battlements as she watched events unfolding below. Immediately, Gilbert seized Blanche in his arms expecting her to yield to him, but she recoiled in disgust, thrusting him away from her. At that moment, Ralph de Capo glanced upwards and thought he saw his enemy and his mistress in a passionate embrace. Ralph took up his bow and fired at Gilbert de Clare, and although his aim was spot-on, the arrow glanced off de Clare's armour, veered sideways and came to rest in Lady Blanche's heart. She fell dead at Gilbert's feet, the arrow quivering in her chest and her beautiful gown stained with ugly blotches of dark red blood. Her ghost is said to haunt the castle today.

Simon de Montfort, who instigated the attack on Rochester Castle, later convened the first directly-elected parliament in the whole of medieval Europe and is held up today to be a hero for his forward-thinking strategy.

The River Medway from the castle today.

GREED AND CORRUPTION

In the 1270s, the Hundred Rolls complain about a certain Richard de Clifford at Gillingham. He acquired £10 from the local people to sow Crown Property lands, but instead of carrying out the task, he kept the money for himself.

AN HORRIFIC EXHUMATION

The statuette of *Our Lady of Gillingham* is said to have rested in a niche in the west door of the Church of St Mary Magdalene at Gillingham Green. There is a fascinating story about her and her opposite number in Chatham. However, it may be myth rather than a true event and it has not been possible to date the story.

It is claimed a corpse drifted in on the Medway, and had to be buried in Chatham. Our Lady of Chatham had been horrified at the corpse's horrible visage so she commanded the clerk to exhume it and toss it back into the Medway. If he refused, she declared, she wouldn't work any more miracles for the parish. So the clerk did as he was told, and the corpse eventually drifted down to Gillingham, and was buried in the churchyard.

However, it turned out Our Lady of Gillingham was just as squeamish as her counterpart in Chatham. She left Gillingham in great disgust, never to return, in spite of the anguished prayers of the parishioners.

JACK CADE – MAYOR OF LONDON?

Jack Cade's real name may have been John Mortimer. He was allegedly of Irish origin, although he grew up in Sussex, and it has been claimed that he murdered a woman there in 1449, which is why he had to flee. After escaping to France, he assumed a false name, Jack Cade, and returned to England. Cade became famous for leading a revolt in Kent in 1450. This is essentially a county crime and the Medway area would have been implicated – it suffered from the punishing taxation just as elsewhere in Kent, while Medway men would have almost certainly been counted among the 20,000 rebels.

Few people would argue that the revolt was anything but just and necessary – Cade's behaviour, however, was disgraceful. The unrest, which had been fermenting for some time, erupted in earnest in the springtime of 1450 when the peasants began to mutter against the corrupt and weak leadership of the King and the unfair taxes levied upon them. Jack Cade produced a manifesto entitled: 'The Complaint of the Poor Commons of Kent'. This was an inventory of grievances against the unpopular government and it included the names of MPs and lords.

In June, 20,000 rebels appeared at Blackheath, including not only peasants but also shopkeepers and artisans as well as the upper-class types, together with soldiers and sailors who had returned from France via the county. Intimidated, King Henry VI took off for safety in Warwickshire, and the rebels advanced on Southwark, where they settled themselves in the White Hart Inn.

On 3 July, the rebel band crossed London Bridge. At this point, Cade got carried away, and, brandishing his sword, declared himself Lord Mayor, and then he led his followers to the Guildhall, then on to the Tower with his demands. The mob captured the Lord Treasurer and speedily beheaded him, and then they went on to decapitate other favourites of the King. Duly spiked in medieval fashion, the heads were then raised in the air and placed together, nose-to-nose, as though they were kissing each other. As if this wasn't enough, Cade and his men started looting, an action contrary to his original promises when he began his march.

THE BARGAIN

By the time they returned to Southwark, preparations had been made to prevent the bloodthirsty rebel from entering the city and, around 10 p.m. a fight erupted on the bridge, which continued until the following morning. The rebels suffered severe casualties and had to retreat. Finally, in response to the Archbishop John Kemp, the Lord Chancellor, Cade agreed to calm his men in return for pardons and fulfilment of his demands.

THE RECKONING

Archbishop Kemp did not follow through. The following week, Jack Cade was to discover a most unpleasant truth; the government now considered him to be a traitor and a reward was out for him, dead or alive.

Cade died in a fight near Heathfield, East Sussex, on 12 July 1450 and his body was taken to London and quartered, the pieces being sent to different cities for display. His head stayed on a pike on London Bridge, along with those of his cohorts. The rebels themselves were pardoned although after Cade's death, thirty-four more were executed. This is a tragic story, since the cause was just and the men were brave – if only it hadn't all gone (literally as well as metaphorically) to Jack Cade's head!

CHANGING SIDES

In January, 1554 it was announced that Queen Mary was to marry Prince Philip II of Spain. Thomas Wyatt, younger son of the famous poet, Sir Thomas Wyatt, decided to join an insurrection against

Left: View of Upnor Castle.

Opposite left: Upnor Castle, detail.

Opposite right: Entrance to Upnor Castle.

the Queen and succeeded in raising an army numbering 4,000 men in Kent. Although troops were sent to deter him, most of them ended up joining Wyatt's army. The soldiers arrived in London in February but found, to their dismay, that Londoners remained loyal to their Queen. Although it was implied that the young Princess Elizabeth was involved in the conspiracy, Wyatt denied this. Ultimately, Thomas Wyatt had no choice but to surrender and he was executed for his treachery.

A CONSPIRACY AT UPNOR CASTLE

In order to protect warships anchored in the River Medway and Chatham Dockyard, Queen Elizabeth I had Upnor Castle built as a gun fort and work began in 1559. Stone to build the castle was taken from the outer reaches of Rochester Castle. William Boume, who was the master gunner, drew up a memoradum, claiming that the large guns were inadequate to protect the castle, and although invading ships might be damaged or demasted, they would not be sunk. It was decided to draw a chain across the river between Hoo Ness and Gillingham to help prevent enemy vessels approaching the castle and action was taken to this effect in 1585 during the war with Spain. It cost £80 a year to maintain by 1588.

However, on 12 June 1667, Dutch vessels gained access despite the heavy chain, although no one knows whether it had broken or was set loose. What is known is that the Dutch were assisted by English soldiers who were angry about low pay and bad conditions at Upnor and who acted as guides for the enemy. When the Dutch reached the Castle on 13 June, they were greeted by fierce fire. Several warships were lost, as well as lives on both sides, although eventually the Dutch were forced to return to Queensborough on 14 June, before repairing back to sea. Instead of the chain, it was decided to build more forts, primarily at Cockham Wood and Gillingham.

SMUGGLING IN MEDWAY

The tiny islands and creeks at the mouth of the Medway provided hiding places for smugglers. The main meeting place of the North Kent gang in the 1800s was based on one of these small islands, Burntwick Island.

Upnor Castle was, reputedly, a fertile ground for smugglers. Since it was poorly maintained, it provided excellent cover for making preparation to smuggle goods to the continent. Some of the smugglers were 'owlers' which meant they smuggled wool out of the country. The militia and the revenue men had a hard time of it when they stormed the Castle because the smugglers always put up a good fight.

Cockham Woods, Upnor is claimed to have been a landing point for smugglers and, of course, Maidstone was actively involved in trying to suppress the practice, and meting out punishment to transgressors. Sometimes even that didn't work because in November 1747 a mob of armed men managed to break open Maidstone Gaol and rescued several dangerous prisoners, having assembled twenty horses nearby to help them escape. The gallows were at Penenden Heath, a mile north of Maidstone, and hangings were described as 'dancing the hempen jig'.

EDWARD ROOTS OF CHATHAM STRIKES AGAIN

In February 1726, two Medway men crossed the Channel to buy 400lb of tea from Ostend, together with some calico and much-prized silk handkerchiefs. Their ship, which carried just seven men, was known as the *Sloweley*. On landing, the goods were transported to a place a few metres north-east of Strood, Northward Hill, where they were hidden in the woods. They completed their assignment by around 3 a.m. and two of the men left while others stayed to

Opposite: A chain was drawn across the River Medway.

Right: Revenue men challenge the smugglers who often put up a good fight. (Courtesy of Richard Platt)

guard the contraband. In the morning, the guards went to the village for food and on returning, having been joined by two others, found the silk and calico was missing. The tea remained, although there were six bags and so the men found it impossible to share out. While they were trying to solve the problem out, the customs men turned up.

We are not sure what happened next, only that no one was ever prosecuted. It is claimed the customs men made a deal with the smugglers, taking some of the bags of tea to sell on themselves. Corrupt deals between smugglers and the authorities were not unusual in those days. Churches were often used for concealing their contraband with the collusion of the clergy.

Like many similar smuggling operations, the venture was masterminded by the infamous Edward Roots.

THE TRAGIC END OF A GREAT HERO

Mounted on a wall of the Guildhall chamber is a large portrait of naval hero and eminent Rochester MP Sir Cloudesley Shovell. Born in Cockthorpe, Norfolk, in 1650, he joined the navy as a cabin boy in 1664, rose through the ranks and became a great benefactor to the city of Rochester. By 1704, Sir Cloudesley was Rear Admiral of England and Commander-in-Chief of the British fleet.

One Sunday morning, 21 October 1704, near the Isles of Scilly, Sir Cloudesley's ship, the *Association*, collided with a rock. Guns were fired to broadcast that the ship was in distress, but the bad weather prevented assistance from other vessels. Although 800 members of the crew were lost, including Sir Cloudesley's wife and two sons, the shipwreck was not responsible for the death of this great admiral.

Sir Cloudesley was one of the first of the victims to be washed onto a cove called Porthellick Bay in St Mary's Island that following morning. But he was discovered by a treasure hunter who

Above left: A portrait of Sir Cloudesley Shovell, town benefactor and murder victim. (Courtesy of Stephen Rayner and *Medway News*)

Above right: A plaque outside the Guildhall commemorating Sir Cloudesley Shovell.

stripped his body of shirt and rings, including an emerald set in diamonds. No one knew this at the time and it was only a number of years after that a dying woman made her confession. She admitted that she found the admiral, exhausted but still alive, and, for the sake of his valuables, she'd committed the terrible crime of murder against this helpless man, a man who had already been through so much. Hoping to assuage her guilt, no doubt, the woman passed the ring to the minister – she hadn't sold it, terrified her crime would come to light.

It is claimed that Queen Anne was devastated at Cloudesley's loss. If you want to see an example of his generosity, have a look at the decorated ceiling in the court hall of the new Guildhall – it was paid for by Sir Cloudesley Shovell.

PIE POWDER COURTS

A charter granted Rochester the right to hold markets and fairs, for example, a three-day fair on St Dunstan's Day, 19 May, and another on St Andrew's Day, 30 November, while the corn market took place every Tuesday. The rear of the King's Head was the venue for yet another market and here a pillory was erected (Epaul Lane, previously known as Apple Lane). Yet another regular market was held on Fridays beneath the Guildhall. Butter, poultry, pigs and vegetables were sold there.

The popularity of these fairs in the middle ages brought in a great number of people and with them, extra problems with disputes arising among the traders, as well as riots, brawls and other

The Justice Tree Stone at Rochester where Pie Powder Courts were held.

disturbances. The fairs were only permitted in areas where there was some authoritative figure to keep order, like a governor or a sheriff. As a result, the Pie Powder Courts came into being so that they could adjudicate on offences committed within the fairground. Pie was formerly spelled 'pye' from the French words, *pied pouldre*, i.e. 'itinerant trader.'

The site of the Butchers' Market was replaced by the Corn Exchange in 1698. In the eighteenth century, a problem arose in narrow Rochester High Street, and gradually traders' goods began to congest the street so that the city council was impelled to introduce special regulations to curb them. Apparently, butchers were the main offenders so their activities were curtailed by forcing them to use only the Butter Market at certain times to sell their wares. Naturally, a few rebelled and in 1731, a Mr Holliden was brought to task for 'drying his skins', which caused a nuisance and made a bad smell.   Eventually, in 1783, the Mayor of Rochester began to plan for a cattle market to help reduce the problem. Subsequently, this market was held on the fourth Tuesday in the month.

BORSTALS

In 1895, it was decided by the Gladstone Committee that youths should be imprisoned separately from adult male prisoners and so the first 'borstal' was established in the village of Borstal in 1902. An interesting detail is that Sir Evelyn Riggles-Brise, who was a prison reformer, was also the governor when the famous Victorian writer, wit and socialite, Oscar Wilde, was imprisoned in Reading Gaol for homosexuality.

The aspiration of the Borstal Prison was originally that of education, discipline and reform but sadly, these institutions made it easy for bullies and psychopaths to indulge their perversions.

2

MEDWAY'S HORRIBLE HULKS

Prior to 1775, many criminals were transported and England was able to rid herself of many a headache. The sentences of transportation started during the reign of Elizabeth I and these felons provided cheap labour for the American colonies.

However, the American War of Independence in 1776 put a stop to that and so the British prisons became seriously overcrowded. It was decided to ease the problem by housing the inmates in outdated warships, soon to be known as 'prison hulks', and so two disused vessels, the *Censor* and the *Justitia* were moored in the Thames at Woolwich. These were specially assigned to convicts sentenced to hard labour. It was only a matter of time before further prison hulks were set up at Chatham, as well as at Sheerness, Portsmouth and Plymouth. Towards the end of the 1700s there were more than sixty hulks in service. They became a fact of life in Medway for some time and one of the most terrible prison hulks was the *Brunswick,* moored off Chatham. Whether on the Thames or the Medway, conditions on the hulks were ghastly. The *Brunswick* accommodated 460 prisoners and it is claimed they were crushed into a deck measuring 125 x 40ft with a ceiling a mere 4ft 10in high.

Convicts were fed boiled ox-cheek, pease, bread or biscuits. Occasionally there was oatmeal or cheese or a couple of pints of beer. Otherwise their only drinking fluid was badly-filtered river water, while their meat was putrid and their biscuits mouldy. Bathing was prohibited and there was precious little soap, resulting in vile skin diseases. Many of the men suffered with diseases of the lungs. Despite their miserably inadequate diet, lack of hygiene, rats and other vermin and accompanying depression endured by these prisoners, they were also forced to slave long hours and provide amusement for tourists who liked to visit to watch them working.

In 1776, a reformer, John Howard, visited the hulks and managed to have some changes made which improved the quality of the food. It was impossible to allow friends and families of convicts to give them food parcels, as saws and other escape equipment would be hidden inside the parcels. Disabled convicts were allowed to grow vegetables, but these found their way to the tables of the officers, not the convicts so in need of extra nourishment. A hospital assistant-surgeon, a Mr Alexander Blyth, was employed first at Chatham, then later at Woolwich. Despite not being qualified, he earned £100 for serving on a hospital ship, and had to take time off (four months every two years) to attend lectures with a view to gaining his diploma.

Eventually, during the mid-nineteenth century, the hulks became obsolete.

TRANSPORTATION

Eventually, an act was passed to allow transportation once again of convicts and on 13 May 1787, 778 convicts (586 male and 192 female) were transported to New South Wales. They arrived in January, 1788, although some died during the journey due to the horrible conditions. Sadly, many wives and children of convicts were left without support and petitioned desperately for the reduction of their

Rainham riverside. Who could believe the terrible prison ships were once anchored on these peaceful waters?

menfolk's sentences. However, few of these petitions were successful. In spite of all the hardship, some prisoners actually made beautiful artifacts out of raw materials like hair, bone and straw.

In 1853, penal servitude, which means imprisonment with hard labour, was substituted for transportation, although it did not come into effect immediately. The convicts at Chatham helped build the naval dockyard. They were luckier than convicts in some other prisons, in that they were given a better diet because of their important labours. The 'extras' included tea with milk and sugar and suet pudding!

HORRID HILL

There's a long, thin promontory, or causeway, extending into the Medway estuary at Rainham's Riverside Park. At the top of the causeway is a low mound called Horrid Hill, which gets its name from the hulks moored nearby during the Napoleonic Wars. These held French prisoners in atrocious conditions, and the confined quarters meant the men also suffered from smallpox, cholera and typhoid. Those who died from these terrible diseases were buried on Deadman's Island and Prisoners' Bank. Sometimes the convicts tried to escape from the prison ships onto Horrid Hill, but the unfortunate men who were caught were swiftly hanged to warn others. Charles Dickens wrote about the hulks in his novel *Great Expectations*, and his colourful character, Magwitch, was the escaped convict who turned out to be Pip, the central protagonist's secret benefactor (Horrid Hill was also a good place for smugglers.)

Prior to transportation, most male convicts were kept on prison hulks, but not all of those sentenced to transportation were actually transported in practice. Female convicts were never imprisoned on the prison hulks.

Looking across the Medway Estuary. Horrid Hill can be seen in the background to the left of the photograph.

SPARE MY CHILD

On board the ship *Fortitude* at Chatham in 1834 was twenty-three-year-old Henry Holland from Mansfield, Nottingham, who was convicted of stealing a horse belonging to a Mr Waterhouse. Henry Holland had been sentenced to transportation for life (Some male prisoners were housed on hulks prior to transportation).

His family petitioned on his behalf, saying that he had never committed any crime before and that the family was honest and industrious. Henry's employer, a 'gentleman farmer' also vouched for him as having been a 'steady, industrious' land servant for six-and-a-half years. Despite further heartbreaking pleas from Henry's mother, 'O pity my situation and spare my child, spare my child', the petition failed. Henry Holland was transferred from Chatham to the *Bengal Merchant* which sailed for New South Wales on 27 September 1834.

On 14 July 1857, the last of the hulks, the *Defence,* was destroyed by fire and the occupants were fortunate to escape from the burning vessel. The fire was thought to have been started by a prisoner smoking a pipe, although tobacco was banned on the vessel. Timbers from the scrapped hulks were used to build houses in Chatham and Gillingham. After seventy-five years, a cruel and barbaric method of dealing with felons came to an end and new prisons were opened in Chatham and Rochester.

Even so, a prisoner's life was far from easy. St Mary's Prison at Chatham was built, but was often described as Chatham's 'hellhole'. There were also other new prisoners, including at Rochester, while Maidstone was the location of the large county prison. There was plenty of room for everyone.

3

TRANSPORTATION

Men were transported for crimes that might seem quite petty to us today, for example for stealing a ewe, beef, a sovereign or lead pipes. Here are some case histories:

A BUSHEL OF BEANS

At the Rochester Sessions on Tuesday 19 January 1830, Henry James Rapley was accused of stealing 16 bushels of beans from Mr John Stunt of Gillingham, the previous 26 December at St Nicholas.

Mr Stunt had sold 12 quarters of beans to a Mrs Ballard at the Bull Inn and this consignment was sent from his Hartlip Farm to Rochester on 20 December. As they approached the Star Inn, the waggoner and his mate were accosted by Rapley who wanted to know where they were going. They replied, 'To the Bull.'

Henry Rapley then informed the waggoners that only 10 quarters of the beans were for the Bull and that he had paid for 2 quarters to be sent to Mr Huggins on St Margaret's Bank. The waggoners believed Rapley and so they delivered just 10 quarters of the beans to the Bull and then proceeded to Mr Huggins with the wagon containing the remaining 2 quarters of beans.

The scam came to light a few days later when Mr Stunt applied for payments for the 12 quarters of beans, only to be told by Mrs Ballard she'd only received 10 quarters. So Mr Stunt challenged the waggoners and discovered what had taken place. He called for Henry Rapley to be apprehended.

The prisoner was sentenced to seven years' transportation, while Mr Huggins had to pay Mr Stunt for the 2 quarters of beans.

FOURTEEN YEARS FOR A HAT!

On Tuesday 21 December 1830 at the Kent Winter Assizes, George Raddall appeared for stealing a hat from Thomas Bennett on the King's Highway in Strood. The sentence was transportation for fourteen years.

SEVEN YEARS FOR STEALING CUTLERY

Samuel Ward also appeared at the Winter Assizes accused of stealing six forks and five spoons, the property of William Heron at Chatham. Samuel received a sentence of seven years' transportation.

TOUGH TIMES

These were tough times generally, even for those not sentenced with transportation. On 10 August, 1830, various persons were brought up to receive sentences which included sheep-stealing, horse-stealing and house-breaking. The paper recorded in its final paragraph that sentences of death were recorded on most of these unfortunate felons.

4

FOOTPADS AND HIGHWAYMEN

During the sixteenth, seventeenth and eighteenth centuries, footpads and highwaymen were a constant threat on Kent roads and in some areas their presence continued into the nineteenth century. This crime has actually been around since the fourteenth century, although no one used the term 'highwaymen' until the seventeenth century. A highwayman was also described as a 'Black Robin', a name possibly derived from Robin Hood of Sherwood Forest.

One of the most notorious spots for highway ambushes was Gads Hill, near Rochester. At this point, the road goes uphill, thereby slowing down the carriages. Not far from Medway is the Swale town of Sittingbourne and this is where a famous Drury Lane actress, Mrs Dora Jordan, was held up by two highwaymen in 1802. Luckily for the actress, her manservant managed to see them off without benefit of Dora's money and jewellery. The actress was later to become the mistress of the future King William IV.

Because highwaymen and footpads were constantly on the move, they posed a big problem for the parish constables; also, they were helped out by publicans, who were happy to play the role of 'fence'. After the 1830s, footpads took over from the highwaymen; they were able to work in twos or threes, so that one could ambush the victim, while his associate(s) carried out the robbery. Occasionally, attractive girls were used as decoys.

One of Kent's famous highwaymen was John 'Swift Nick' Nevison although, confusingly, John was also known as William. The name, Swift Nick, was coined, allegedly, by King Charles II out of admiration for John Nevison's exploits. It is believed he was probably born near Sheffield around 1640 into a well-established, wealthy family. He had a reputation at school for getting into trouble, mostly through being 'lightfingered'. Later, he came to London and was employed as a brewer's clerk, but on collecting a debt, the enterprising scoundrel absconded with the money to Holland. Then he joined up, distinguished himself in Flanders serving in an English regiment under the Duke of York. When he returned to England, apparently he lived with his father until the latter died. Now John Nevison was without means and this was when he made his decision to become a highwayman.

THE ROMANTIC IDEAL

Perhaps, though, this particular highwayman deserved the well-used and flattering title 'Gentleman of the Road'. John was always charming, it is claimed, and never used violence to achieve his ends. Women adored him and he was, apparently, always kind to the poor and only took from those who could spare it.

Various romantic stories arose about highwaymen and it is difficult sometimes to know which are true. It is reported that he had a gang of six outlaws who met in Newark and robbed travellers along the Great North Road, also that he robbed a boy in Gads Hill, Kent and rode 200 miles to York in a day, where he talked to the mayor, thereby providing himself with an alibi (This story has also been attributed to Dick Turpin).

Highwaymen once terrorised travellers in Medway country lanes.

ESCAPE AND ARREST

It seems that after being arrested for horse-stealing and robbery, he escaped gaol twice, once in 1674 (from Wakefield) and once in 1676.

In 1681, John Nevison was arrested again and the cunning felon arranged for an accomplice to impersonate a doctor and pronounce him dead from the plague. The scam worked and again, John escaped. Then two brothers, called Fletcher, tried to arrest him and died in the attempt. Bounty-hunters found him after a tip-off having a drink at the Magpie Inn at Sandal near Wakefield and this time, he was tried and condemned and then he had to face execution. At forty-five years old, John 'Swift Nick' Nevison was executed at York Castle on 4 May 1684. He was buried at St Mary's Church, York.

THE DREADED GIBBET

It is not recorded what happened to John Nevison's body after he was executed. However, the punishment for highway robbery could be severe and the authorities used their corpses to act as a warning. The felons were hung from the gibbet complete with their fine wigs. Tar would be applied to their bodies to prevent them from rotting, just as happened with smugglers. The last recorded case for highway robbery was about 1838, nine years after the Metropolitan Police were established in 1829, subsequently implementing horse patrols on Kent's main roads.

5

RICHARD DADD

The life of Victorian artist Richard Dadd was full of contradictions. He was a painter of fairies, the leader of a clique of talented artists and an insane asylum inmate. And, finally, a murderer, for Dadd stabbed his father to death while in the grip of insanity.

So what drove a talented young man with good prospects, described by contemporary journalist and editor, Samuel Carter Hall as '... tall with good and expressive features and gentlemanly demeanour' to commit the terrible act of patricide?

EARLY LIFE

Richard was the son of Robert Dadd, a respected chemist born in Brompton in Chatham in 1798. On 5 November 1812 Robert married Gillingham spinster Mary Ann Martin and Richard, their fourth child, was born in 1817. Sadly, in 1823, when Richard was just seven years old, the young mother died, but within a couple of years Robert remarried, this time to Sophia Oakes, aged eighteen, with whom he had two more children. In 1835, Sophia died so it can only be imagined what effect the deaths of these two young mothers must have had on Richard and the other children.

Richard would have been fairly streetwise, as children were in those times, and familiar with the rougher aspects of a dockside town, its inns and places of ill-repute, its squalor, drunkenness and violence. However, he also developed a keen affection for nature, from the coastal and riverside areas to the lovely Kent countryside. This sense of place found its way into Richard's art.

In 1836, Robert Dadd decided to move to London and here Richard pursued his artistic career, being admitted to the Royal Academy School, and he was soon accepted as a full student and supported by other prominent artists.

THE TURNING POINT

According to some biographers, Richard Dadd's travels may have influenced his soundness of mind. Through a mutual acquaintance, David Roberts, Richard was introduced to Sir Thomas Phillips, of Newport, Monmouthshire, a solicitor and mayor of the town who had been knighted by the Queen. Sir Thomas was planning a grand tour around the world and needed a companion. Richard Dadd was delighted when Thomas Phillips invited him to accompany him and the two set off on 16 July, 1842.

Through his letters, three of which were addressed to David Roberts, we learn something of Richard Dadd's state of mind at this time. In Venice, he became indignant about the exploitative behaviour of the greedy gondoliers. He respected money but feared chaotic, unruly crowds which produced a tension in his mind.

Richard Dadd – nervous depression led to derangement.

Later, he complained of other cities and their inhabitants, of knaves and cheats and the inadequacies of their priests. As his travels continued through many strange places, including Corfu, Athens, Damascus, Jaffa and Jerusalem, he became increasingly bewildered at the villainous behaviour he encountered, the filth and the squalor. Unsurprisingly, there were incidents of threatening or hostile behaviour from the locals, and he was continually upset at the 'madness' and the 'dirt'. So distressed was Dadd by these distractions that he complained of being unable to draw and even admitted he doubted his own sanity and had become prey to 'nervous depression.' It was clear that his mind was beginning to crumble; one of the most frightening aspects was a sudden urge to attack the Pope in Rome. Dadd's sense of self-preservation, fortunately, overcame his weak-mindedness and prevented him – the Pope, he decided, was too well-protected. Later, it was claimed his derangement may have been due to sunstroke, although this seems unlikely given the long period of instability and the fact that symptoms of his condition had occurred prior to his travels.

A LITTLE HELP FROM HIS FRIENDS

Previously, around 1840, Richard Dadd belonged to a little group of young artists known as 'The Clique' who used to meet in rooms in Soho for discussing future plans and for mutual support and debate. Among them were Dadd's closest friends who also studied at the Royal Academy Schools, William Powell Frith, Henry O'Neil, Augustus Egg and John Philip.

When Richard Dadd arrived in London in April of 1843, he decided to enter a competition. The topic was the decoration of the new Palace of Westminster so immediately Dadd began to seek a room which would serve as a studio for working on his cartoon. Augustus Egg seems to have been the first of the friends to recognise Dadd's symptoms of insanity. He told his friend, the painter, Frith, and broke down as he tried to describe Richard Dadd's condition. Later, when Dadd himself arrived at Frith's address, he seemed fine, cheerful and talkative and Frith decided that Augustus Egg was mistaken.

This impression did not last long. Soon all the friends observed the horrible downturn as Richard Dadd began to lose his struggle between reason and madness. He came to harbour feelings of persecution, imagining he was being 'watched,' and living on eggs, ale and little else. His cartoon, St George after the Death of the Dragon did not attract favourable criticism, but, in general, his creativity remained unaffected as he continued to produce beautiful works of art.

A CUT-THROAT PURCHASE

During the last week of August 1843 we know Richard visited Mosely & Co., Cutlers, of New Street, Covent Garden. Here he bought a cut-throat razor and a clasp-knife. Meantime, his father, Robert, who was becoming concerned about his son's mental state, consulted Dr Sutherland at St Luke's Asylum. On Saturday 26 August Richard was examined and he was deemed not responsible for his actions. His father, Robert, however, was in denial and the following day, became convinced his son was getting better.

A TRIP TO COBHAM

It is not surprising then, that the following day, Robert and Richard Dadd planned a trip to Cobham together so that Richard could have a heart-to-heart with his father. They took the steamboat from London to Gravesend and made their way to the High Street where they engaged a gig for Cobham, arriving at the Ship Inn at around 6 p.m. John Adams, a waiter, told them there were no beds available at the inn, but managed to acquire two beds at separate cottages in the village.

Robert and Richard went out for around one hour, returning at 7 p.m. for supper. Then, as reported by John Adams, Richard asked his father to go for a walk with him. Robert was unenthusiastic, it was now around 8.30 p.m. dusk was falling and he was tired. Richard left his father for a while to get a glass of water from the bar, and then he returned to his father and repeated his request that Robert accompany him for a walk.

Despite encroaching darkness, they walked through the park and around the hall. Eventually, around a quarter mile from the hall, close to a chalk pit, Paddock Hole, Richard attacked his father with a terrible, desperate violence, using the razor and the knife. Then he tried to drag the body away, perhaps intending to dispose of it, but eventually, he had to give up and, leaving his father for dead, Richard Dadd climbed a stile and ran away. (After this terrible deed, Paddock Hole was known as Dadd's Hole, but the hole has since been filled in due to road widening.)

DISCOVERY

Robert Dadd's body lay face-down around 30ft from the road, but at first it was not clear whether he was dead or maybe a dozing drunk. So Charles, nephew of butcher Abraham Lyster, was not unduly alarmed when he spotted him from the gig. The two men were on their way to Wrotham Market and, staring at the body, they discussed whether it might be someone who would attend the fair at Strood. They called to the man, and when he did not reply, Charles Lyster went to investigate. Realising that the man was dead, he called out to another man in the distance, George Biggs, a shepherd. Charles Lyster and George Biggs turned over the body and, seeing the awful mutilation, realised the man had been brutally murdered.

George Biggs remained to guard the body, while the Lysters went to report the murder to the constable in Cobham. Then the Lysters continued on to Wrotham and the constable, William Dawes, hurried to Paddock Hole to examine the body. Robert Dadd's black coat, once unbuttoned, revealed congealed blood and there were deep wounds to the throat and chest. Nearby Dawes found the knife and later, the razor was discovered beneath Robert's corpse.

After leaving the body at the wheelwright's shop in the village, where it was later identified by John Adams, William Dawes informed Chatham and Rochester authorities of Richard Dadd's crime, with orders to find him. A further search was implemented by Mr Morrison, a Steward of the Earl of Darnley, throughout the park. But Richard Dadd could not be found. He had fled by post-chaise to Dover and got himself across the Channel to Calais, explaining his dishevelled appearance as being due to an accident. He purchased a new suit and abandoned his blood-stained clothes at the Calais Inn. Then he took a train to Paris.

MEETINGS WITH DEVILS

Richard Dadd began to have a conversation with the other occupant of the carriage and, fairly soon, became convinced his fellow-traveller was possessed by the devil. It was Dadd's mission to kill the devil and, desperately, he peered out of the train window into the skies, searching for a sign. He decided that if the setting sun completed its task without a cloud in sight, the man would be spared, otherwise he must be killed. Luckily for the man, the sun sank into cloudless oblivion.

A further 'bargain' was made while travelling in a diligence through the Forest of Valence. Again, there was one other passenger, a Frenchman. Again, voices bade Richard Dadd to kill his travelling companion. And again, his fevered mind looked for a sign to guide him, and this time he searched for an answer in the stars. If Osiris moved towards its neighbouring star that would be his trigger and the man should be killed.

In due course, Richard Dadd moved towards the Frenchman, lowered his cravat and collar, while drawing from his coat a cut-throat razor. Naturally, the Frenchman resisted but was unable to overcome Dadd before receiving four wounds to his throat.

THE INSTRUMENT OF GOD FACES HIS INQUISITORS

Richard Dadd appeared before the JP in Montereau, and willingly provided all the information required, his name, his crime against the Frenchman and the killing of his father. Accordingly, he was transferred to the asylum at Clermont, Fontainebleu, still believing himself the instrument of God, commissioned to destroy men possessed by the devil. He swore the killing of his father was a good act, for he had destroyed an 'enemy of God'.

Also on Dadd's list was the Emperor of Austria, Ferdinand the First.

In England, the post-mortem had returned a verdict 'Wilful murder against some person or persons unknown.' Robert Dadd's funeral took place at Gillingham Church and because of its sensational aspects, was full to overflowing.

As soon as the story of Richard Dadd's flight and arrest came to light, George William, Richard Dadd's younger brother, who had also showed signs of insanity, was admitted to Kensington House Asylum. He was only twenty years old and although his behaviour was harmless, merely delusional, no one wanted to take any risks after what had happened with Richard. Meanwhile, Richard's health worsened in the French asylum, but eventually he improved and was sent back to England in 1844.

Maidstone Prison, where Richard Dadd was committed one year after murdering his father. (Courtesy of Richard Platt)

THE GAOL, MAIDSTONE.
KENT.

Richard Dadd at work. (Courtesy of Marc Demarest)

CREATIVE GENIUS – FAMILY SHAME

On Monday 29 July, Richard appeared before magistrates in Rochester, in a long beard and moustache, but he refused to offer any defence. After a further appearance in court, he was committed to Maidstone Prison, then, around one year after the murder, on August 22, he entered the Criminal Lunatic Dept. of Bethlem Hospital. He was, at this point, aged twenty-seven. With the support of the authorities, he continued to paint successfully during the next forty-two years of his life. Some of his work was used to decorate the asylum, although this displeased his family as it promoted public knowledge of their relative's bizarre and shameful situation.

6

TOO BEAUTIFUL TO DIE

So – how did Elizabeth Law get away with it? Elizabeth was just eighteen years old in 1855 and lived in Chatham where she worked as a lady's maid to seventy-eight-year-old widow, Catherine Bacon. She'd got the job when her mother, Isabella Law, who sold fruit, heard about the vacancy.

Elizabeth Law appeared at the West Kent Quarter Sessions, Maidstone on Friday 16 March of that year. She was accused of murdering her employer, Mrs Catherine Bacon of No. 11 Ordnance Terrace, on 29 January 1855. Throughout her appearance in court, Elizabeth wept into her little white handkerchief, looking helpless, vulnerable, appealing and heartrendingly innocent. All of that counted for a lot, since there were no female jurors, the entire jury being comprised of small tradesmen. The prosecutor was a Mr Bodkin of Bodkin and Denman.

Elizabeth's plea was clear and uncompromising. 'Not guilty'.

Catherine Bacon had been brutally cut down by a hatchet murderer and no one could possibly believe that sweet Elizabeth was that murderer. Carefully, Elizabeth explained to the court that Catherine had been attacked by two men who had knocked on the door on Monday morning 29 January (at this time there was no council refuse collection and men would call with a donkey and cart to remove household rubbish for a small fee). Elizabeth explained how one of the men, the younger one, pushed past her. Mrs Bacon, a fragile woman who weighed no more than 4st, was coming downstairs. The younger dustman seized the screaming Catherine and forcibly projected her down some stairs into a cellar. Then, whispered Elizabeth, the other man, the older one, pulled her into the kitchen and took liberties with her. According to Elizabeth, after the younger man had finished killing Catherine, he dragged the body up to the first floor bedroom and the older man drew his knife across Elizabeth's throat and pushed her to the ground.

ANGEL LOOKS – A DEVIL'S HEART

But some things just didn't add up. For example, with all that screaming, you'd think the neighbours might have heard something. It was also very strange how much Elizabeth knew about the hatchet when she was purportedly in another part of the house. Besides all this, the police established there was no one else in the house at the time except for Elizabeth Law. She must have done it! A number of other matters came to light. Elizabeth was unreliable, she stole, sneaked out at night to rendezvous with unsavoury characters, and she especially loved men in uniform.

On the day before the murder, she got herself 12s by pawning Mrs Bacon's satin gown. Then she went up Pump Lane with boyfriend John Swinyard and got drunk with him in his room. In spite of getting back late, she was up on time next morning and chopping wood as the weather had been severe recently with heavy snowfall. Then Catherine approached Elizabeth and began to complain about her behaviour, accusing the maid of 'sneaking out' when her back

Right: Front elevation of Chatham's Theatre Royal.

Below: Back elevation of the old Chatham Theatre.

River Medway at Chatham.

was turned, but Elizabeth denied the charges. It made no difference because Catherine gave her notice. Elizabeth was furious.

She raised the hatchet high above her head then thrust it down into the old woman's skull. There was blood everywhere, all over the victim and all over Elizabeth as well. Frantic to conceal her crime, Elizabeth washed Catherine's face and body and removed her dress, hoping death would be ascribed to natural causes once the blood was removed. She also took Catherine's ring and brooch and then carried the emaciated body upstairs.

There was a knock on the door. Quick-thinking Elizabeth Law drew a knife across her own neck, drawing blood, before she opened the door to the two small boys. As though she was unable to speak, she pointed upstairs to where the body lay.

Dr Gammie was summoned from No. 5 Ordnance Terrace and he said that Catherine's body was cold but not rigid so she must have died about one hour earlier. He found it strange that the face had been washed and asked who did it. Elizabeth decided to brazen it out and said, 'I did it.' The case was further investigated by PC Howes and Supt Everist, who unearthed further inconsistencies, for example, the jewellery taken by Elizabeth Law. Then, after investigating the area downstairs, a horrible discovery was made in the privy – Catherine Bacon's blood-soaked dress. In Elizabeth's room, her own dress was discovered, full of pawn receipts in the name of Rebecca Pocock.

In spite of all this damning evidence, the jury still couldn't bring itself to convict the lovely young thing in the dock so, to the horror of the prosecution and police, she was found not guilty of murder. However, the court did manage to impose on her a six-month sentence

Man dressed in uniform of a Victorian undertaker. (Dickens Festival, summer 2007)

with hard labour for theft. As for the murder, which everyone knew full well Elizabeth Law had committed, she got off scot-free, since she could not be retried for the same offence. An interesting fact is that Charles Dickens lived in the house thirty-five years previously. Catherine and her husband Matthew had moved in during the early 1820s.

7

THE BRUTAL MURDER OF A YOUNG MOTHER

In 1894, Joseph William Ellis Holgate was probably the most hated man in Medway. Joseph and his well-liked but shy twenty-eight-year-old wife, Grace, had been married for five years. Grace was the mother of one child, a son named Willie, and was heavily pregnant with another. She'd had a bad time with her first pregnancy, having suffered from debilitating epileptic fits.

Instead of showing his young wife the support and compassion she deserved, Joseph Holgate behaved like a brute. One day during the last week in July 1894, Holgate decided it was time to look at the household accounts. When he was unable to reconcile the figures, he began to blame Grace. 'That's fifteen shillings out of the pound I gave you,' he yelled. 'What have you done with the rest?' When Grace tried to explain, he called her a liar. The quarrel continued to erupt over the next few days and on the following Tuesday, Mrs Charlotte Baker, a neighbour, heard their little son screaming. Peering in the window, she could see Holgate's hand raised as he fiercely beat Grace, all the time swearing at her. Mrs Baker told how Grace had been crying out in pain.

Later, on another occasion, another neighbour, Mrs Emily Packham, heard the usual loud arguing accompanied by violent banging, and then saw Grace run from the house and return a few minutes later. Grace could not bear to leave her little son behind and had returned for him. She told Holgate she was leaving with Willie.

Now Holgate became inflamed with anger and grabbed hold of her and dragged to her front door, challenging her to '... take me to the police and have me locked up.' As she tried to get away, he hit her twice in the face. Somehow, the terrified woman managed to get hold of her son and escape from the house in Copenhagen Road. She hurried towards her stepfather's house in Britton Street. But Holgate was at her heels. He followed her into the house.

Grace's stepsister immediately asked a neighbour, Mr Henry Dixon, to help, then the two of them went upstairs where they found Holgate with his hands around Grace's throat. 'You won't hit her while I'm here,' Mr Dixon told Holgate. This just made Holgate even madder. 'I'll knock her head off,' he shouted and then he hit Grace as hard as he could and she was hurled against the wall.

A DYING WOMAN'S PLEA

Somehow, Mr Dixon managed to eject Holgate from the house. All the time the brutal man was trying to justify his actions, declaring that no one knew what he had to put up with. Once they'd got rid of her husband, Grace was put to bed but, unsurprisingly, what with the pain both mental and physical, she was unable to sleep. Grace was in a critical condition, cut and bruised and, of course, pregnant. When she was questioned by a police officer, Grace said, 'Joe's hurt me, but he's my husband. Please don't lock him up.' A doctor was summoned and immediately, he had her taken to the Medway Union Infirmary. Then Grace suffered a particularly debilitating epileptic fit, no doubt brought on by the trauma. As she lay dying, her second son was born – he was dead.

Above: An old photo of Gillingham Park where Grace may have walked with her son, Willie.

Right: Most hated murderer – Joseph Holgate. (Courtesy of Stephen Rayner and *Medway News*)

The post-mortem failed to determine exactly what had caused her death, the beating or the fits. All the same, the jury agreed unanimously that her husband's violent attacks had accelerated her critical condition. He was committed for trial on a charge of manslaughter, later altered to unlawful wounding and grievous bodily harm. However, when the prosecution's case was heard, the Judge, Baron Pollock, said this was as cruel a crime as any he had ever heard of. Holgate received a sentence of penal servitude for ten years.

A further incident related to this story occurred shortly after the murder. That August afternoon in 1894, Holgate went to stand by his wife's graveside thereby causing a riot amongst the furious women of the town, who chucked dirt and stones at him – and anything else they could get their hands on to pelt him with. Holgate had to be speedily removed from the cemetery by carriage and still the women pursued him through the streets of Gillingham. In the High Street, they chased him into the Railway Hotel shouting abuse. He tried to escape from a side door, and finally in Skinner Street, they caught up with him and began beating him with their umbrellas till he was rescued by police and taken to the station where he was charged with striking his wife.

8

PRISON – A BREEDING GROUND FOR CRIME

These were the days when prison meant punishment rather than a secure environment for felons with a view to reforming prisoners and reintegrating them into society. Prison conditions were foul and its inmates treated like low life. After 1815, Fort Clarence was used as a military prison and lunatic asylum. It was built between 1808 and 1812 in St Margaret's Street, Rochester, to prevent invaders crossing between the Maidstone Road and the River Medway. Later, asylum patients were moved to a new hospital, but the prison remained and it is recorded that reports of floggings appeared in the local newspapers.

St Mary's Dockyard Prison was frequently described as a 'hellhole' and conditions at Borstal were extremely hard, causing many young men to try to escape. Of course, a few of them were hard, criminal cases, while others were just unfortunates. The Borstal Institution was built in 1902 by convicts working at the Dockyard and the stone buildings were inhospitable and often freezing cold. No wonder so many tried to get away.

DEATH WAS HIS FRIEND

Long-term grudges are frequently the cause of violent flare-ups and the case of prisoner James Fletcher, aged twenty-three, was no exception. An inmate of Chatham's St Mary's Dockyard Prison in 1866, he'd just been given two days' solitary confinement after warder James Boyle, reported him for swearing at another prisoner. Convicts at St Mary's who were reported for misconduct were sentenced to bread and water for a certain number of days, according to the severity of their crimes.

Unbearably lonely and fed up with the meagre rations, Fletcher emerged from his solitary cell only to be set to work with his fellow prisoners, smashing at rocks with hammers in the punishing heat of a warm September day. Fletcher 'lost it' and turned on the warder Boyle – smashing into him instead of the rocks. The blow was fatal and it is noted in the *Chatham News* that no other convict came to the aid of warder James Boyle, so he must have been very unpopular. A fellow officer tried to help by attacking Fletcher and stabbing him, but not before he'd dealt the hated warder three blows with the hammer.

James Boyle suffered for three days, before finally losing his tenuous hold on life. Fletcher recovered to face his executioner. Already, he had a record having been sentenced to seven years hard labour for highway robbery with violence. In spite of his many assertions of cruel treatment of the prisoners, for example, having to eat candles and soap to supplement their miserable diets, Fletcher didn't stand a chance. He was speedily found guilty and sentenced to death, but this wasn't a problem for Fletcher. He'd always made it clear that death would be his friend.

Grave of Edward Adams. (Courtesy of Stephen Rayner and *Medway News*)

A CRYING SHAME

Unlike the above case, another prison warder, Edward Adams, aged fifty-three, was a kind, reputable man who simply got in the way of his charge's ambitions for escape. Edward Adams worked at the Borstal Institution in Rochester and had thirteen years experience in the job. Edward sometimes felt pity for those kept here under lock and key and this proved his undoing.

Frederick James Smith (real name Cullender) was a thief and a shop breaker and due to his long record of criminal convictions, was sent to Borstal in June 1919. He was also misbehaving and as a consequence was punished several times. He was awaiting trial for destroying institution property, but the young felon's mind was always busy plotting his escape. On Friday 2 January 1920 at around 7 p.m., Smith started making a loud noise in his cell, so kindly Edward Adams succumbed and allowed him outside to help clean the corridor. Smith had already ascertained the alarm bell wasn't working.

He stole up behind the older man who was working on his report at his desk and hit him on the head with a scrubbing brush. Edward Adams fell off his chair and crumpled to the floor. Smith got the keys out of Adams' pocket and grabbed a broom. Opening the door to the yard outside, he was soon over the wall and away, making his way through the Borstal village and onto Wouldham, then Burham, hugging the river.

The old Rochester building shortly before refurbishment (2006) part of the former HMS *Pembroke* site, now occupied by the universities.

Eventually, he was cornered by two policemen in a cart shed at Burham Court Farm in the middle of the night and he was taken to Malling Police Station. The following Tuesday, Smith and another inmate, William Ernest Scutt, aged seventeen, also arrested that morning, appeared at Rochester's Guildhall. An ironic footnote to the story of the young men's journey to Maidstone Gaol, having been remanded in custody, was that they passed Edward Adams' funeral between Borstal and St Margaret's Cemetery. Adam's funeral was attended by men from HMS *Pembroke* as well as fellow prison officers.

Smith was found guilty of wilful murder. While they were considering their verdict, the jury put forward some harsh criticism to be referred to the Home Office about inadequate regulations at Borstal in respect of discipline. After this, the evidence seems a little confusing. Smith claimed the escape was a mutual venture which included Scutt, but the latter denied he had any part in Smith's plans. Scutt was not helped by the fact his clothing was found bundled in Smith's cell. Conspiracy seemed likely but the prosecution was unable to prove this and Scutt was acquitted. Smith refused to say anything in his own mitigation.

On went the judge's black cap and Mr Justice Avery pronounced the death sentence and the execution date was set for Tuesday 9 March. An appeal achieved a postponement, then a reprieve was granted on Saturday 13 March. The prisoner's mother, who lived in Bermondsey, was informed that the death sentence on her son had been reduced to life imprisonment.

9

THEY GOT OFF SCOT-FREE

Sometimes, in spite of every effort, certain crimes remain unsolved although police and neighbours sometimes have a pretty good idea of who might be responsible. Here are two horrible crimes from the Medway area for which no one was ever convicted.

THE REVD 'SHERLOCK' JORDAN

A horrible murder in Hoo, St Werburgh, was never solved by traditional methods, although a feisty vicar did his best to put matters right after the investigations of the professionals had failed. The murder happened in Hoo St Werburgh, right under the Revd Richard Jordan's nose, on Sunday 11 December 1808. A parishioner, William White, was shot dead while sitting at his living-room fire at Cockham Farm. William White, who died instantly, was the owner-occupier of the farm.

It was clearly a carefully premeditated plan, since, during the hours of darkness, the murderer had set up a hurdle as a gun rest in the garden of the farmhouse, so that he was able to shoot straight through the scullery window. It was thought the murderer was a man with local knowledge, since he knew William White would be sitting right there on his own. By choosing the Sunday evening, the murderer also ensured that no domestic servants would be around to bear witness against him. Also, he positioned his gun on the hurdle exactly at 8 p.m., so that the sound of gunfire was obliterated by the customary volley of shots from the convict hulks lying nearby on the Medway.

After the deed, the murderer disappeared into the darkness with the murder weapon, to hide it in a barn where it was found some time later. William's corpse was discovered within a matter of minutes by his children. It must have been heartbreaking to see them crying over their dead father. George White, the eldest son who, it was claimed, had designs on the farm, was suspected, especially as he'd been heard threatening his father. However, the twenty-four-year-old explained to the Bow Street Runners that he had an alibi and couldn't possibly have done it. He had been in Hoo Village between 7.45 p.m. and 8.15 p.m. which was at least one mile from the farmhouse. Apparently everyone believed him, and the Bow Street Runners who had hurried to Hoo to make their investigations, eventually admitted defeat and decided not to pursue their questioning. An open verdict was recorded by the Rochester coroner.

But Revd Jordan wasn't going to let it go and, convinced George White was the murderer, determined to break the unmarried, eldest son's alibi. On the 26 January, Jordan preached a fiery sermon and then he placed a book in the vestry and demanded each male parishioner enter his name and a statement of where he was at 8 p.m. on 11 December – and this entry was to be witnessed by another person. Then Jordan presented a broadsheet requesting information about any strangers in the area at the time. The next item on the agenda was questioning the villagers and this began on March 9. Jordan was thorough.

On March 26, Jordan told George White to call a vestry meeting in order to clear himself of suspicion for the murder of his father. On Easter Monday, 3 April, after a dinner for forty at

The church at Hoo St Werburgh, where amateur sleuth, Revd Richard Jordan solved a murder. (Courtesy of Stephen Rayner and *Medway News*)

the Bells Inn followed by a meeting to settle parish accounts, Jordan insisted on George White making a public statement. He quickly proved that George had left the farmhouse at 6.50 p.m. to walk to Hoo but he did not turn back to fetch a handkerchief from his bedroom as he claimed. Instead, he'd gone into the garden and set the scene for murder. If he'd had had a handkerchief at the time of his father's death, he would have wiped his eyes with that instead of with the back of his hand. Revd Jordan was also able to prove George had not bought a bag of nuts at the village shop at 7.45 p.m. because the vicar had found a witness who saw him cracking and eating them at 7.40 p.m. Also, George claimed to be standing at the Bells pub when the hulks' guns were fired, but in fact, that had taken place fifteen minutes earlier.

Further, he had not arrived at the vicarage until 8.20 p.m. and, as the vicar's housekeeper claimed, his breathing was laboured when he got to the vicarage door. George had had ample time to carry out the murder of his father and then double back to the village. But George White never went to trial. Knowing he was beaten, George took off and emigrated to Australia, saving himself from arrest but also losing his inheritance.

AN OUTRAGE IN SNODLAND

The brutal murder of a thirty-seven-year-old policeman, PC Israel May in 1873, has never been solved. When his body was discovered in Snodland in a field, it was clear that he had put up a

Israel May's grave. (Courtesy of Stephen Rayner and *Medway News*)

desperate fight for his life, and the struggle had covered an area from the road, through a hedge and into the field. The policeman's head had been battered and it is claimed his truncheon was missing, the assumption was drawn that it had been used as a murder weapon. What makes this case particularly bizarre and rather poignant is that PC May's cries were actually heard – by another *policeman* – at about 2 a.m. Since the other policeman had, a short while ago, helped two drunken soldiers onto the Burnham ferry headed for Snodland, he assumed they were the ones making the sounds.

At the inquest held at the Bull, Snodland, the body was shown to the jury. Gradually, throughout the proceedings, the pattern of PC May's movements was established – but not the identity of his killer. Mrs Selina Upton was the last person, except for the murderer, to see the policeman alive and she was a beerhouse keeper's wife from Ham Hill in Birling. She'd hailed PC May from her bedroom window at about 1.30 p.m. on the Sunday morning of the murder. Selina Upton then described how she heard PC May talking to a local man, Mr Kelvie, who was driving a horse and cart down the road. PC May was remonstrating with Kelvie and his boy for driving along while asleep and insisted on helping lead the horse to avoid it doing any damage.

What happened between this incident and the dreadful killing of the policeman can only be guessed. A bricklayer, James Stone, and an acquaintance passed along the road around 6 a.m. and saw another man, Walter Imms, staring at something in the field. The two men went to look and Stone's companion, William Middlemist, went off to find PC May! At this stage, no one could

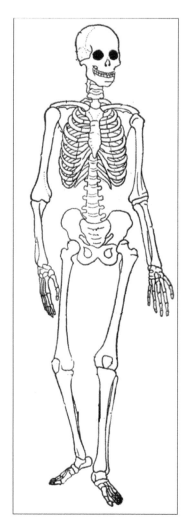

A human skeleton.

identify the horribly battered body, which was lying partly on its face and partly on its side, until, eventually, Mr Furley, the turnpike gateman, went to look and claimed it was PC May. Both the policeman's hat and the attacker's cap were found near the hedge, together with a tobacco box, braces and handcuffs. There was blood everywhere and footprints going towards the road.

Finally, Supt Hulse of the Malling Police Division arrived and had the body taken to the Bull Inn. At the inquest, Supt Hulse expressed his intention of catching the murderer and bringing the case to a satisfactory conclusion. Unfortunately, the jury had to return a verdict of 'wilful murder by some person or persons unknown', and the murderer was never captured.

WHO MURDERED EMILY TRIGG?

In 1916, for around twelve weeks, a woman of twenty by the name of Emily Trigg worked as a maid at No. 36 Maidstone Road, Rochester, for Miss Catherine Cooper. Miss Cooper was very happy with Emily, who was smart and respectable. On Sundays Emily went to tea with her mother in Providence Road, Bluebell Hill. So, on Sunday 6 August, she put on her Sunday best outfit, which consisted of a blue dress and white, rose-sprigged hat. Although she left around mid-afternoon, Emily never made it to her mother's, nor did she return to the house of Miss Cooper. The latter assumed Emily wasn't well and had stayed over at her mother's. The following Tuesday, Mrs Kate Trigg got in touch to find out what had happened to Emily, and it was only then the two women realised something was seriously wrong. Emily had vanished.

The police were informed, but they were unresponsive. This took place during the First World War so there were more pressing matters to think about, what with Zeppelin raids and absconding servicemen. It was only when the body was discovered six weeks later that anybody, apart from her mother and mistress, took any notice. A Rochester greengrocer, John Jennings, and his family were in Bridge Wood by the Maidstone Road, collecting blackberries. The little family found much more than just a few berries for pudding – a few yards into the woods they discovered a human skeleton, its skull still showing hair and an imitation-diamond comb. The little rose-sprigged hat and a necklace which had fallen nearby was also identified as Emily's. Some of her clothes had been ripped off and lay in a pile a short way from the body.

Sickeningly, it looked as though Emily had been choked to death, for there was some material in the skull of the skeleton, as though it had been forced into Emily's mouth while she was alive. This was only guesswork – it was not possible to be sure choking was the real cause of death. There was little else to show and it was mentioned how quickly the body seemed to have decomposed, leaving little to go on.

Emily's boyfriend, George Harris, who was a private in the Royal Surrey Regiment, was picked up as a suspect, but soon eliminated. He had been in hospital in Shoreham at the time of the murder. There was also a story that Emily had been seen with someone in military uniform that afternoon and she had also told Miss Cooper about a meeting with a soldier. So maybe she was seeing someone else besides George.

Emily's inquest was adjourned until 9 October to give the police time to make enquiries, but no further evidence came to light. Supt A.E. Rhodes, in charge of the investigation, reported that all the investigations had produced no further leads. The jury returned a verdict, 'Found Dead'. Strangely enough, ten days later another man was arrested, a gunner in the Royal Garrison Artillery at Winchester, by the name of Charles Hicks. Hicks was held in prison till the following Tuesday, but was discharged for lack of evidence.

HANGED BY THE NECK UNTIL YOU ARE DEAD

Imagine what it would be like to know that tomorrow morning a grim-faced jailor will arrive at your cell door to escort you to a place of execution, where a rope will be placed around your neck while you stand on a removable platform. The only person on your side will probably be the prison chaplain or minister. The executioner, especially if he is of the ilk of the awful William Calcraft, wants to make an exhibition of your painful death, perhaps for the benefit of others watching as well as for his own twisted satisfaction. In other words, he wants you to dance for him. If you are being hanged before public hangings were abolished, then you may be providing entertainment for an enormous crowd of spectators.

Imagine this was you. How would you cope? The following Medway case histories demonstrate a variety of reactions, terror, apathy, even one or two who actually welcomed the forthcoming experience.

I DESERVE TO DIE

In the early 1800s, Duncan Livingstone was a busker of sorts and liked to dress up in Scottish national dress and play the bagpipes in the street for money. His helper was a small boy with a tin mug who collected the cash for the performances. One day, however, the little boy went missing and later his body was discovered. He'd been horribly murdered. Livingstone was immediately suspected, since he was known for having a violent temper and also for indulging in bouts of drunkenness. However, Duncan Livingstone was nowhere to be found and a reward was offered for his capture.

Some time later, a carter gave a lift to a destitute-looking man who'd accosted him close to Gad's Hill, Higham. The carter was sure it was Duncan Livingstone, so he took the frightened man to the authorities at Gravesend, where the cart was headed. He received a reward of £100, which, it is claimed, he wasted on drink, eventually being killed beneath his own wagon. The venue for Livingstone's trial was Rochester's Guildhall, which was then a courtroom. Livingstone confessed and further, agreed he deserved to die.

LEARN FROM MY FATE AND GOD BLESS YOU

Crowds came to watch the spectacle of the unfortunate man's execution taking place at the cattle market (the site is now occupied by the popular Rochester Friday morning market). The Vicar of St Nicholas Church, Revd Barrow, attended the condemned man, then later, a Calvinist minister, stepped in, a Mr Thomas Drew of the Zonar Chapel, Strood. At noon on 3 February 1820, Livingstone got into the wagon with the jailor and executioner and was followed by the dignitaries including the mayor and town clerk, in an open carriage. This entourage was

Right: An etching of a hanging by Goya.

Below: The River Medway viewed from Strood.

also accompanied by policemen on horseback. Soon, the little column wended its way to the place of execution. With the rope around his neck, Duncan Livingstone asked permission to speak to those who had come to watch him die. He told them to learn from his fate, caused by drunkenness. As the cap was pulled down over his face, he cried 'God bless you all!'

Fortunately for him, Duncan Livingstone seems to have died quickly and was buried that night close to the castle wall.

A HORRIBLE ASSAULT

According to the Rochester Gazette of 10 August 1830, Thomas Surtus was charged at the Maidstone Assizes with having violently and feloniously ravished and carnally known Sarah Taylor against her will. This nasty assault took place in the Parish of Strood. Thomas Surtus was a seaman on board a coal smack which traded between Shields and Strood.

A servant at a farmhouse in Cuxton, Sarah had been sent to Rochester to make purchases for her master. On her return to Cuxton, she noticed a man was following her, and, to her discomfort, had begun to overtake her. He muttered a few words to her and then he seized her violently by the arms. He dragged her from the path and into the standing corn, forcing her to keep quiet by threatening to 'rip you up with my knife.' Then Surtus committed this horrible capital crime on the young woman.

The next day Surtus went into fields in the same neighbourhood and tried to assault another woman, an act that led to his apprehension. He was carrying a long, clasp knife with which he intimidated his unfortunate victims.

The jury reached a verdict of guilty and the judge put on his black cap and passed sentence of death, as reported by the newspaper 'in a very serious manner.' Thomas Surtus was executed at Penenden Heath on August 24, leaving a wife and one child.

BUTCHERED FOR NINE SHILLINGS

Chatham lad, fourteen-year-old John Any Bird Bell is said to be the youngest person ever executed at Maidstone Prison. Along with his small accomplice, his eleven-year-old brother James, John Bell murdered a thirteen-year-old boy, Richard Taylor, in woodlands in Chatham. This horrible act was motivated out of greed.

On 29 July 1831, a Friday, with his brother standing as witness for the prosecution, the jury heard that Richard Taylor was the son of a poor tallow-chandler living in Stroud (Strood). The previous 4 March, Richard Taylor, wearing his sou'wester, blue jacket, waistcoat and brown trousers, was sent to Aylesford to collect a weekly parish allowance of 9s, for his disabled father. He was an intelligent boy of amiable disposition, the court was told, and he had carried with him a knife so he could make himself a bow and arrow on his return journey.

The relieving officer of the parish, a Mr Cutbath, reported paying Richard the usual sum of 9s and this Richard hid away in a small bag which he carried in his hand inside a mitten. He had run this errand for his father before, but this time Richard did not return home and as darkness fell, his father became anxious. The next day, Mr Taylor set off to Aylesford to find his son and discovered that Richard had duly collected the money. However, there was still no sign of the young boy.

On 11 May, a man called Izzard was walking along a path in the woodland, around two miles from Rochester and close to the high road. Mr Izzard made the distressing discovery of Richard's badly decomposing body, lying in a ditch. After the authorities were informed, it was found that the clothes were disarranged and the mitten cut away, indicating there had been some sort of fight. Blood from a wound around the neck area suggested he had been cut by a sharp instrument. Soon, a search was underway to find the weapon and this turned out to be a common, white, horn-handled knife, although by now it was badly corroded. The constable began investigations. Since the Bells, the father and two sons, John and James, lived in a poorhouse close by where the murder was committed, it wasn't long before the knife was correctly attributed to the elder Bell son, John.

WITNESS TO AN EXHUMATION

A further investigation was made into the circumstances of the murder, necessitating the disagreeable task of exhuming the body as it had been buried soon after discovery. To see what effect this exhumation would have upon the boys, they were taken to the graveyard to witness it. John remained silent and impassive. James was asked to empty the pockets of the corpse and this he did with surprising good grace. He handed over the knife lent to Richard Taylor by his father when he'd set out on his errand.

The two boys were closely examined by the magistrates and finally the younger boy confessed that he and his older brother John were responsible for Richard's horrible death. James explained that he had kept watch while his elder brother waylaid and murdered Richard. Eventually, John, too, confessed and the court was horrified by the depravity of the two boys who had planned the murder ever since learning the reason for Richard's excursions to Aylesford. James received 1s 6d from his brother for his contribution to the deed. John Bell was found guilty of the wilful murder of Richard Taylor and the jury did not even need to retire to reach their verdict. Sadly, a plea for mercy in view of John Bell's youth failed to save him. All the same, John Bell maintained a stiff upper lip throughout his trial, appearing both indifferent and unafraid. He expressed no guilt for his crime, although he became a little emotional when he was told his body would be donated to medical research.

AN AUDIENCE OF THOUSANDS

He was sentenced to be hanged at 11 a.m. the following Monday, 1 August 1831, outside the prison gate. Five thousand people turned up to witness the spectacle. A 'New Drop' scaffold had been erected, as was usual the day before an execution. Imagine John Bell's horror at the sight of the platform, supported by those sturdy, heavy beams. In the centre, inside the railings, there would be a gallows of two upright beams and a cross-beam complete with an iron hook where the noose was attached. An integral part of the platform was, of course, the lethal trapdoor.

John Bell would have had to climb the steps to his death. Once the executioner had done his job, the lower body of the victim would be obscured by the black cloth hanging below the platform so that the spectators would not see the struggling torso and legs of the felon, a small Victorian concession to good taste! This type of gallows was used until the 1880s.

Afterwards John Bell's body was passed over to the city of Rochester's surgeon for medical dissection.

No resting place for John Any Bird Bell – this old burial ground is now the Town Hall Gardens at Chatham – the tombstones are lined up against the outer wall.

THE ULTIMATE IN FORGIVENESS – SARAH ANN PENFOLD

On the morning of 4 June 1898 Sergeant Burr was summoned to a lodging house in Queen Street just off the sleazy Brook district. He was taken to a bedroom on the second floor, where the body of a naked women lay over a chair, her face bloodied and bruised. She had a wound on her chest and her limbs were badly bruised, while splodges of blood littered the walls. Items of clothing were scattered around as though they had been torn from her. Thomas Daley was the boyfriend of the woman whose name was Sarah Ann Penfold and apparently she'd left her husband and two children to be with him seven years previously.

Sarah Ann Penfold was thirty-eight and was described by a police superintendent, rather patronisingly, as 'a superior person of her class'. She was generally known to be quiet and law-abiding so Daley's comment, 'She came home drunk last night and fell down,' was unconvincing. Thomas Daley was forty years old and he worked sporadically distributing handbills. He was not well-liked.

It was clear to Sergeant Burr that Sarah had been struck repeatedly in a frenzied attack with a poker, fire shovel and chair. Her attacker had then jumped on her and kicked her, before tearing off her clothes. Amazingly, after all this, he'd actually gone to bed and enjoyed a good night's sleep. Even more amazing, no one in the lodging house had come to investigate or called for help. As one neighbour, Charles Grant, said, 'It's a common occurrence in the Brook. If she'd shouted 'murder' I would have got up.' Another neighbour, Ann Bailey, confirmed she'd heard the woman being beaten all night, and her groaning becoming fainter. The coroner enquired if she'd thought to doing anything to help and her response was that the couple were strangers to her. Such for community spirit in the Brook during the late 1800s.

When Daley stood up to give evidence, he said he could not kiss the Bible, as this would be a mockery in view of his crime. He then explained to those gathered in the Medway Union Workhouse how Sarah had got back late after going out on an errand. When he asked what had happened, she told him she'd been drugged by some people who'd then tried to get her into a house. She said she'd recognise them again, and then she fell down, so her head was against the fireplace. Daley tried to persuade her into bed, but she refused, so he stripped her and forced

During Victorian times the Brook was a place of ill-repute. The photograph shows Charles Dickens' house.

The Brook today.

her into bed. She kept getting out, upsetting a jug of water in the process. Daley was irritated and he picked up the poker, striking her and knocking her to the floor. Gradually, after a couple of kicks, it dawned on Daley he had killed his wife. He dragged her onto the chair, then went to bed, still drunk.

When he was making his statement, Daley began to praise Sarah, saying she was the best woman who ever lived, but that she was led astray. Thomas Daley was sent for trial at Maidstone Assizes, the date set five months later in November. Unfortunately a witness was missing; the aforementioned Charles Grant had earned himself a year's hard labour that very day for robbery with violence. A plea of 'temporary insanity' was put forward, but the Judge, Sir Henry Hawkins was having none of that. Drunkenness was no excuse for crime, he insisted and Thomas Daley was found guilty of murder by the jury, who did not even bother to retire to discuss it. Daley was sentenced to death and hanged in Maidstone Prison.

SOME SOBERING REFLECTIONS ON HANGING THROUGH THE AGES

At the beginning of the nineteenth century, death by hanging was a matter of course for a range of serious and petty crimes, including theft. Sometimes the death sentence was reduced to transportation or imprisonment. Thirty-seven prisoners condemned at Maidstone's Spring Assizes in 1801 had been guilty of sheep stealing, burglary, highway robbery and murder. Four of these were hanged at Shooters Hill, fifteen were hanged at Penenden Heath and the remainder were reprieved. Three young men were hanged for arson at Penenden Heath in 1830. The following year a scaffold erected at the new Maidstone Prison made Penenden Heath redundant.

CHILDREN

In the eighteen and nineteenth centuries, children and young adults suffered the death penalty for crimes such as murder, property crimes, highway robbery and arson.

It is claimed that Michael and Ann Hammond, brother and sister, were the youngest children to be executed in Britain. They were just seven and eleven years old and they were hanged at Kings Lynn on 18 September 1708 for theft. It was reported that it thundered after the hanging and Anthony Smyth, the hangman, died a fortnight later.

RELEASED FROM THE JAWS OF DEATH

Although the following is not about Medway, it's worth relating as it describes the suffering experienced by those who are hanged. John Smith was hanged at Tyburn on 25 December 1705, but he did not die and after fifteen minutes the crowd shouted for him to be cut down. He was taken to a house of safety where he shortly recovered and he was able to describe his experience. This is what he said, and no doubt others have experienced the same although few survive to tell the tale.

'When I was turned off I was, for some time, sensible of a very great pain occasioned by the weight of my body and felt my spirits in strange commotion, violently pressing upwards. Having forced their way to my head I saw a great blaze or glaring light that seemed to go out of my eyes in a flash and then I lost all sense of pain. After I was cut down, I began to come to myself and the blood and spirits forcing themselves into their former channels put me by a prickling or shooting into such intolerable pain that I could have wished those hanged who had cut me down.'

THE BODYSNATCHERS

In 1540, Henry VIII ruled that surgeons would be allowed four bodies each of executed criminals per year. Medical schools at this time were desperate for dead bodies so that their surgeons could dissect them to learn about anatomy and improve their skills. Prior to 1832, unless the court had ordered otherwise, the criminal's body was usually given up to family or friends. After 1834, it was decided that the bodies of the executed belonged to the Crown.

Convicts working at Chatham Dockyard. (Courtesy of Stephen Rayner and *Medway News*)

MAKING AN EXAMPLE

Before 1834, the horrible practice of gibbeting or hanging in chains could be ordered by the courts to make an example. After hanging, the prisoners were stripped and dipped in tar. Once it had cooled, they would be placed in an iron cage which was riveted together and hung from the gallows or sometimes from a specially built gibbet erected in a prominent place like a crossroads or maybe at the very top of a hill. This gruesome sight acted as a warning to people, helping to keep them in line. Sometimes the bodies remained until they decomposed or were eaten by birds.

The criminals most likely to be ordered to be gibbeted were highwaymen, murderers or pirates.

THE END OF A BARBARIC SPECTACLE

On 29 May 1868, Parliament passed the Capital Punishment within Prisons Bill ending public hanging altogether in Britain. All future executions would take place within the walls of prisons. On 26 May, 1868, Michael Barrett, who'd tried to blow up Clerkenwell Prison, was executed – and his was the very last public execution. His crime had killed four passers-by and a number of people were injured in the explosion. Three of his accomplices were acquitted before Barrett died before a crowd of 2,000. The first private hanging was carried out at Maidstone Prison two months later when a Dover railway porter was hanged for murdering a stationmaster at Dover Priory. (See *Dover – Murder & Crime,* by Janet Cameron for the full story.) But hanging wasn't actually abolished till the 1960s.

II

NATURE OR NURTURE

Here is a case that doesn't fit in anywhere else in this book – it's just too weird! It's about a young man with a truly bizarre ambition – while other young men of those times wanted to be soldiers or sailors or train drivers – he just wanted to be a murderer. He longed for the sensation of feeling a noose around his neck. More than any other case, the story of Robert Burton makes the reader question whether it is pure evil or an insane obsession that incites a young man to such brutal behaviour.

THE STRANGE OBSESSION OF ROBERT BURTON

Robert Alexander Burton was an eighteen-year-old apprentice who, on 11 April 1863, was publicly hanged by the short-drop method. Burton had wanted to join the Forces and managed to join the West Kent Militia in Maidstone. However, he soon deserted with his bounty money and began employment with a shoemaker. Soon, he was up to his old tricks and stole from his employer and as a result, was imprisoned for two years.

This strange young man, who'd first wanted to be a soldier, (and then changed his mind) now decided he wanted to be a murderer. He desperately wanted to experience the feeling of the noose around his neck. He thought the shoemaker who'd shopped him would be a good start, but the man had already moved out of the area. There was, on the other hand, a barmaid who'd refused to serve him in a Chatham pub, but she was a feisty woman and Robert Burton thought she might make too much trouble.

So Burton picked on someone smaller. Thomas Frederick Houghton was only eight years old (or nine years old, in some reports). Burton saw the child with his mother talking to a baker's boy, and he followed them home. Thomas's mother went indoors while the child remained outside to play on the Lines. It was about 2 p.m., Tuesday afternoon. Burton followed Thomas then went up to him and knocked him down. He dragged him, struggling, towards one of the airshafts ventilating the London, Chatham & Dover Railway Tunnel which passed under the Chatham Great Lines, an open area of land. Then he got out his knife and cut the little boy's throat, severing his windpipe. Thomas continued to struggle and, later, Burton complained that he did not 'die quickly enough.' So he knelt down and put his hands around Thomas' throat until blood ran from his mouth and nose and he knew he was dead. Then Robert Burton went to the military bathing pond and washed his hands, face, clothes and knife clean of blood. He hid the knife in a WC of a house behind the Dark Sun pub in Chatham High Street.

CONFESSING THE HORRIBLE DETAILS

On Wednesday, 23 July, 1862, a PC Hibbert was confronted by Robert Burton who said he was confessing to the murder of Thomas Houghton and willingly spelt out all the horrible details.

Chatham High Street today.

Looking towards Chatham town centre
from Fort Amherst.

Hibbert took Burton back to Rochester Police Station and discovered the murder had been committed the previous afternoon. Burton led the police to the scene of the crime. The little boy lay on his back, arms bent, throat cut, his face and arms covered in blood and bruises on the side of his face. He was though to have died around 2.30 p.m. His body was taken to the Napier Arms and a post-mortem confirmed it was the throat wound which was fatal.

Burton said he was weary of life and determined to kill someone, no matter who. At the Spring Assizes, there was a large and angry crowd waiting outside the court and Burton was heard to remark that they (mostly women) deserved the same as the murdered boy. He pleaded guilty to murder but then there was an attempt to change to a defence of insanity as there was a history of mental ill-health in the family. This was not accepted as his mental state was not sufficient under the M'Naughton Rule. (See below).

Robert Burton was convicted and sentenced to be hanged by the neck until he was dead. Politely, he thanked the judge and three weeks later, on 11 April 1863 he was despatched at Maidstone Gaol by the executioner, William Calcraft. He gave himself up to death without a struggle, smiling with pleasure.

THE M'NAUGHTON RULE

The M'Naughton rule (sometimes described as the right-versus-wrong test) was derived from the 1844 trial of Daniel M'Naughton who was accused of killing the British prime minister's secretary. He had thought he was actually shooting at the prime minister. The defence claimed that M'Naughton was not responsible for his actions due to insanity. The M'Naughton rule states that '... individuals cannot be held criminally responsible for their actions if at the time of the offence either 'they did not know what they were doing', or 'they did not know that what they were doing was wrong'.

TWO FOR THE PRICE OF ONE – VICTORIAN STYLE

James Fletcher was hanged for battering to death with a hammer, warder, James Boyle, while being held in a Chatham prison in 1866 (see page 46). However, Fletcher had some female company during his death throes. A jealous woman, Ann Lawrence, aged twenty-nine, had been separately tried for murdering her four-year-old son and then attempting to kill her lover in Tunbridge Wells in a fit of rage after a quarrel.

Both Fletcher, aged twenty, and Ann Lawrence were convicted at the Winter Assizes, December, 1866, and so, William Calcroft despatched both to their deaths on 10 January, 1867. The double-execution was for the purposes of convenience and cost-cutting. There was only one set of gallows to be erected, as well as paying wages for only one set of guards, a useful saving! William Calcraft may have been persuaded to do two hangings for the price of one, and, in addition, would have been able to reduce his travelling expenses.

12

MAKING THE PUNISHMENT FIT THE CRIME

We can find a number of parallels between crimes today and yesterday's counterparts. It was just as dangerous to drive a cart carelessly in the 1800s as speeding in a Ferrari today – people still end up being killed. Today criminals are more likely to steal identities or bank account details than rabbits. Although the reasons behind criminal activity are mostly easy to understand, for example, vengeance or profit, sometimes the felon's true motivation can actually seem rather strange or misguided. Here are some crimes that would be rather differently interpreted today.

ALL FOR A LOAF OF BREAD

At the Kent Winter Assizes of Tuesday 21 December 1830 John Thomson was accused of obtaining 30lbs of bread with intent to defraud Thomas Weekes of Chatham and he received one year in the House of Correction and Hard Labour.

THE RABBIT ROBBERS OF ROCHESTER

Five labourers, Walter Chatters, Charles Moore, Charles Warren, Sucker Gough and Joseph Brown were accused of assaulting a boy, George Merrit, and stealing three rabbits on 31 December, 1869. The alleged offence took place on the Rochester/Maidstone Road. The pilfered bunnies belonged to a Mr E.R. Coles, who was, according to the *Chatham News*, one of the magistrates on duty that day. Mr Coles retired from the bench for the duration of the hearing.

Young George Merrit described how, the previous Friday, he was taking eighteen dead rabbits along the high road leading to Maidstone. They had been left in his care by some gentlemen who were still out shooting. On reaching the second milestone, seven men approached George, asking him the way to Chatham, but then they surrounded him. 'Who do those rabbits belong to?' they demanded. George Merritt informed them they belonged to gentlemen who were out shooting in the woods.

'Let's have some,' said the men, but George explained that the dead rabbits were not his. The men ignored him and instead several of them picked up rabbits from the ground. George began to shout for help, then Walter Chatters struck him violently on the back with a stick. Frightened, George ran away and when he returned, he found the men had disappeared – and so had five of the rabbits although later he found two on the ground nearby.

George Merritt confirmed that he recognised the prisoners as five of the seven men who had accosted him. All the men, he said, had sticks and this was confirmed by an eye-witness. The assistance of Sergeant Hinds ensured the eventual apprehension of the five men. The newspaper noted that six nets and a rabbit were recovered from Charles Warren at the police station.

Chatters continued to insist that the boy, George Merritt, had spoken falsely on oath, while Moore declared he had never touched a rabbit, and had told the others not to touch them or they would get into trouble. Warren said he picked up a rabbit, but put it down again quickly after Moore's warning. Gough and Brown also denied touching the rabbits.

The Bench retired and when they returned, the mayor said the charge of a felony against the prisoners was withdrawn, but they would be 'proceeded against' on a charge of assault on a boy. The prisoners pleaded not guilty and again the evidence given by George Merrit was read out by the clerk. Chatters repeated that the boy spoke falsely – he had never struck him!

The mayor considered the evidence, deciding that there was a violent assault on the young boy and Chatters was fined 30s, including costs or one calendar month's hard labour. The other men were fined 1s or, in default, fourteen days hard labour.

FURIOUS DRIVING

On 30 July 1870 the City Magistrates at Rochester heard a summons against Joseph Edwards for furiously driving three horses drawing a carriage along the High Street, Rochester on 13 July. Edwards pleaded guilty.

Mr Searles, a fishmonger, reported that he saw Edwards passing his shop 'at a rapid pace' and a friend commented the driver wouldn't go far without meeting with an accident. He was right. As the defendant drove near Eastgate, his carriage was upset and he and his friend went sprawling into the road. His carriage had collided with a brewers' dray standing at the doorway of a Mr Fairbairn. Another witness, Dr Gunn, confirmed the truth of these statements.

Mr Levy, who was sitting on the bench, was said to own the dray, which he denied. However, it was acknowledged that this was a bad case and that Edwards was 'known for furious driving.' The defendant apologised and was fined 10s and 13s costs.

A SPREE WITH A COCKEREL

Alfred Spree, a youth of fifteen years, was charged by Mr A. Murphy, an inspector of the Branch Society for the Prevention of Cruelty to Animals, for ill-treating a cock on Sunday 31 July, 1870, as reported in the *Chatham News* on Saturday 6 August. The case was heard at Rochester.

Mr Murphy explained how he was passing by the corner of Mill Lane, Ordnance Place, about 3.30 p.m. on Sunday. Hearing a noise of voices coming from the Brewers Arms beerhouse yard, he looked through the fence. He saw the prisoner and two other boys watching two cocks fighting so he jumped over the fence and seized one of the birds. The accused boy claimed it belonged to him. Mr Murphy asked him why he was fighting the bird and Alfred said he actually brought it to the Brewers Arms to sell it.

Several people interceded, promising the bird would be killed if only Mr Murphy would take no further notice of it. The prisoner refused to give his name and address so he was taken into custody. In court, Alfred told the judge the birds were not 'trimmed' for fighting and he asked for the case to be adjourned so he could summon witnesses *(the author was unable to locate the outcome of the final hearing in the Medway archives)*.

TIN KETTLES – INCITEMENT TO RIOT?

Sadly, a simple marriage celebration was the source of an unpleasant assault on one of the city constables in Troy Town during November 1929. An indictment was found against Mr John Ludlow and Mr John Greenwell Cornwall for a riot and an assault on John Tuff.

A Mr Dives was married to 'a person named Dunstall'. The two defendants found a number of boys to play some 'rough music on tin kettles and other noisy instruments' (*Rochester Gazette*, 20 August 1830). Each young person was offered 1d for his services. The boys assembled around Mr Dives' house and, according to the newspaper report, 'made a riotous noise encouraged by the defendants.'

Mr Tuff was sent for to re-establish order, but he was set upon, assaulted and abused by the two defendants. Mr Tuff called several witnesses to help him prove his case. Mr Shee conducted Ludlow and Cornwall's defence and tried to demonstrate that the boys were merely there to welcome the happy couple, according to old English custom. No riot, said Mr Shee, was committed nor any assault on the constable. However, the defendants were found guilty of riot and assault and both were fined.

13

HARD TIMES

Many of the hearings listed under the police courts involved crimes such as stealing items as diverse as forks and spoons, watches or clothing, being drunk and disorderly, using bad or foul language, or the more alarming such as ill-treatment of a child or an animal, (ass, donkey, horse, goat or cock). Frequently very stiff sentences were handed out for pathetically petty crimes committed by the deprived or hungry, or even by children as young as nine or ten. At other times, there seemed to be a high level of tolerance towards parents who abandoned or cruelly ill-treated their children. Here is a selection of crimes of varying severity which took place between 1830 and 1870.

A PAUPER'S LOT

An inquest in *The Times* newspaper dated 21 January 1837 describes the sad 'riches to rags' demise of a Medway trader. The case was heard in the North Aylesford Union Workhouse in Strood and concerned a trader, Thomas Burton, aged sixty-five.

The first witness was Charles Dean who was the watchman for the parish. He described how on the previous Sunday night, around 11.30 p.m. the Dover coachman told him someone was lying in the road and would most likely be run over. Mr Dean set off up Strood Hill and met the man coming down, staggering drunkenly. Charles Dean led him down the hill, asking him where he was going. The man, Thomas Burton, said he wanted to go to Strood, so Charles Dean left him.

Later, he found Thomas lying in the road again, so he called on a friend to help him and the two of them took Thomas to the Bull's Head where they were able to make him warm and comfortable in the straw. But Thomas wasn't getting better and the men called on James Vine, the relieving officer of the workhouse. Vine, at first, came to the conclusion the man was drunk, although later he conceded that Thomas was really ill.

A man, assumed to be a doctor's assistant, told the court he'd arranged for Thomas Burton to be put to bed and kept warm, and to have beef tea and brandy administered every two hours. But he must not be bathed as that would tire him. So Thomas Burton was returned to the workhouse in a filthy state, and an inmate, Susannah Hayler was employed to wash him with warm water. It was during this process that Thomas died.

It was found that Thomas' pockets contained addresses of upper-class people he thought might help him – and there was other evidence that proved Thomas Burton had formerly had connections with people of substance, for example, there were letters from Lord Cornwallis and the Earl of Jersey. William Stephenson, the medical officer, carried out the post-mortem and found the body perfectly healthy.

But – there was not a particle of food in it. Thomas Burton had been kept warm, bathed, fussed over but it had not occurred to anyone to give him something to eat.

Medway slums.
(Courtesy of
Stephen Rayner and
Medway News)

TWO HANDKERCHIEF THIEVES

On 4 December 1870 Mary Ann Collins, aged nineteen, and Elizabeth Brown, aged sixteen, entered a drapers' shop and pretended to look for dress patterns and materials. Later, they appeared in court at Rochester accused of stealing two handkerchiefs from the shop of Mr Jones, High Street, Rochester. Each young lady was sentenced to twenty-one days' hard labour.

SPIRIT OF CHRISTMAS

The *Chatham News* of 15 January 1870 reported that at the Police Court in Chatham Henry Hall, landlord of the Victory beerhouse in Chatham was summoned for having 'his house open for the sale of beer during prohibited hours on Christmas Day.' He was found guilty and fined 1s with 9s costs.

WILLIAM AND MARY

William Smith and his wife, Mary Ann, were charged with stealing a child's bedcover and a petticoat from a clothesline at New Brompton on 4 January 1870. These items were the property of Mr George Beale, had been drying in a backyard and were eventually missed around 7.00 p.m. (Presumably the petticoat belonged to Mr Beale's wife and, by default, to him!)

Mary Ann Smith called at Mr Randall's pawnshop in Globe Lane, Chatham, that same night, offering to pledge the petticoat for 1s 6d. William Randall, assistant to Mr J. Randall, suspected the article was stolen and detained Mary Ann, shortly giving her into the custody of 'Instructing Constable' Wood. From the information provided, Constable Wood discovered the identity of the owner and went directly to the Travellers' Rest beerhouse on the Brook, Chatham, where the prisoners were lodging. Other property was found in the room occupied by the Smiths, including clothes pegs and the child's bedcover. He took William to the Station and locked him

Left: Old Globe Lane has disappeared, instead nearby are a large car park and the modern Pentagon Centre.

Right: Railway Bridge over Canal Road.

up. Mary Ann had already explained how her husband brought stuff home and sent her out to 'pledge' it, so presumably this is why she was treated more leniently.

Mary Ann was discharged but William was sentenced to fourteen days' hard labour.

A POOR OLD SOUL

Richard Rees was, in the words of the *Chatham News* of Saturday, 22 January 1870, 'a deplorable-looking old man'. Richard was charged with unlawfully begging at Brompton on 15 January. Richard Rees suffered from delusions and believed he'd travelled the circuit with the Lord Chancellor; that he'd been college-educated at Oxford and was, in fact, the best writer in England. He was sentenced to one day's imprisonment. At the same Sessions, two other beggars received five days imprisonment – one of these unfortunate men walked with two sticks and both of them were hungry.

PAY HER ONE SHILLING

According to the *Chatham News* of 26 February 1870 a poor woman named Alice O'Niell appeared at Rochester Police Court. She'd been discovered by a Mr Radley at 12.45 a.m. sitting on a Strood doorstep. As an act of mercy, he took her to the police station – otherwise she may have perished in the cold.

Alice had recently been released from Maidstone Gaol and she had no means of supporting herself. She was walking home to Deptford. The magistrates dismissed her, ordering her to leave the city. Fortunately for Alice, a gentleman in the courtroom gave Mr Radley 1s for the 'poor creature'.

AN IRRESPONSIBLE MOTHER

The *Chatham News* of Saturday 15 January 1870 reported that at the Police Court at Chatham the previous Monday, Eliza Fleming, with a child in her arms, was charged with being drunk and disorderly on the Brook on 7 January 1870. Eliza Fleming was fined 10s and 6s costs.

A CRUEL CASE OF CHILD DESERTION

At Rochester on 5 March 1870 Mrs Vickers, who kept an eating house in the Canal Road, Strood, put in an appearance to ask for some advice from the magistrates. The previous Sunday night, two young ladies passed her shop and found a child aged two years outside. The child had been 'cruelly deserted'.

Throughout the article in the *Chatham News*, the child was referred to as 'it' so we cannot tell if this was a boy or girl. The tiny child was almost frozen from exposure to the cold night air and its clothing was dirty. 'It prattled' continues the paper, 'that it did not want to go home as its mother beat it. But it was pleased with a passing railway train and said it had been in one.'

Mrs Vickers made enquiries through the police and other sources but she couldn't find out who the parents were and wanted to know what to do as she couldn't afford to keep it. The *Chatham News* noted that Mrs Vickers had acted very kindly.

The magistrate told Mrs Vickers that the child could be admitted to the North Aylesford Union at Strood and that the court would approach Mr Saunders, the relieving officer, to this end. The Union would also make efforts to trace the irresponsible parents.

WHO NEEDS ENEMIES WITH A MOTHER LIKE THAT?

At eleven years old, at Chatham on 30 July, 1870, little Elizabeth Bruce was charged with stealing a pair of trousers and an old skirt, valued at 1s 6d. Her accuser was – her *mother*, also called Elizabeth Bruce. The young prisoner pleaded guilty and it is easy to imagine her tears at being so betrayed by the one person who should protect her.

Mrs Bruce said she was a widow who lived in King Street, the Brook. She left for work the previous Saturday leaving her children at home, the eldest being the prisoner, the youngest aged just four years. Naturally, Elizabeth, the eldest, was in charge of the others. Mrs Bruce returned home around 3.30 p.m. and soon missed the items of clothing and asked little Elizabeth where they were. Elizabeth said she didn't know. So the mother asked the younger sister, who told her the prisoner has given the things to her to go and sell, so she took them to Mr Boatman's at the Brook, a second-hand clothes dealer. Mrs Sarah Boatman, the wife of the above, confirmed that on Saturday, she bought the articles produced in court from the girl, Emma Bruce, who said her mother had sent her on the errand.

Mrs Boatman was soundly admonished by the court for not making better enquiries about the provenance of the goods. 'If there was no receiver,' she was told, 'there would be no thieves.' If she ever gave such facilities again to children in the future, she would be in trouble herself. As for the prisoner, the magistrate said he was sorry to hear so bad a character of her and he wouldn't be doing his duty if she wasn't severely punished. The little girl was sentenced to seven months hard labour and afterwards a Reformatory for five years.

14

MEDWAY'S MILITARY HELL ON EARTH

This is one of the saddest stories in this book. It concerns the Darland Glasshouse, which comprised a number of wooden huts near the A2 at Gillingham. Fort Darland, alias the Glasshouse, was a detention barracks which struck fear into the hearts of any soldier who thought he might be sent there. The glasshouse was surrounded by a 12ft-high barbed-wire fence, and within this grim vicinity, soldiers, to be held under sentence, were confined. The Military Provost Staff Corps ensured that the imprisoned soldiers were treated like dirt, abused both verbally and physically, kicked, sworn at, deprived of liberty, tobacco and other army comforts – and made to operate at the double at all times.

THE HELLHOUSE INSIDE THE GLASSHOUSE

Rifleman William Clayton, whose nickname was Sammy, was sent to Darland Glasshouse in 1943. Clayton, like many other soldiers, had difficulty coming to terms with army discipline. At forty, he was deaf, older than most of his compatriots and suffered from breathlessness and chest pains. He'd actually been placed in medical category 'C', not an ideal profile for a fighting soldier. It was Sammy's fourth sentence and this time the MPSC were spoiling to make his life a misery. They saw him as a challenge, someone who needed the stuffing knocked out of him. As a result of their harsh treatment of William (Sammy) Clayton, the unfortunate soldier died.

That last afternoon really was hell on earth for Clayton. As a squad of men doubled across the square, William Clayton had fallen out. On being confronted, he explained to Staff Sergeant James Pendleton, 'I can't march, sir.' He should not have had to make an excuse as the sergeant had earlier reprimanded Clayton for wearing his respirator incorrectly.

NO SYMPATHY

Pendleton handed Clayton over to Regimental Sergeant Major John Culliney and Quarter Master Sergeant Leslie Salter and he was thrown into the single cell punishment block for charge next day. Except that 'next day' never dawned for William Clayton. He'd been killed by Culliney and Salter. Culliney had been furious that Clayton had struggled to get along to his quarters to collect his kit and, believing the prisoner to be malingering, he slapped him in the face, while Salter shoved the kit at him and directed him to the cell block. Clayton was just too slow for them, dropping his kit, nearly falling over. Culliney gave him a hard punch on the jaw, then hauled him into a standing position to punch him again, then shook him while Salter twisted his arm. There were more punches. Oblivious to the blood pouring from his face, the two cruel officers propelled him along by his arm and collar, then, when he collapsed, they shoved him in a barrow to take him to his cell.

Unsurprisingly, Clayton was unconscious by now, so his head was held in a drain to bring him back, but his head was banging on the sides as he was shaken. Then the officers threw water on his face. By now, Salter, at least, was becoming concerned because Clayton's face was bluish grey, his tongue curled to the back of his throat. He looked as though he was dead. They sat him on a chair in the night watchman's room, head bloody and lolling over while his mouth frothed with saliva. Shortly, he was certified dead.

The inquest found that death was caused by tuberculosis exacerbated by the behaviour of the two violent officers, Culliney and Salter. Now it wasn't looking so good for these two monsters as the judge, quite rightly, pronounced that if death had been accelerated by even a few hours, then that amounts to manslaughter. Consequently, the two men were found guilty at their trial at Kent Assizes, when Mr Justice Humphries said, 'I believe that Culliney lost his temper and behaved in a brutal way towards a man believed to be malingering and I think Salter, to some extent, acted under orders. This sort of conduct cannot be tolerated.'

A CHANGE FOR THE BETTER

As a result, Culliney was jailed for eighteen months and Salter was jailed for a year, with loss of rank and no prospect of pensions. But the case had deeply shocked the public and investigations were put into force to see whether this sort of cruel treatment was administered regularly to prisoners. Penal standards were demanded and it was pointed out that the War Office should not merely conduct its own enquiry. Sir Winston Churchill demanded an investigation into 'the supervision and administration of discipline, medical care, training, welfare, accommodation, feeding and the suitability of staff' and this was to take place in naval and military prisons and detention barracks. As a result, there were changes made for the better, and, ironically, the MPSC (Military Provost Staff Corps) were renamed 'Murderers of Poor Sammy Clayton.'

15

MILITARY MAYHEM

ROOM NO. 34

During Nelson's time in the 1800s, a sentry with a peg-leg and crutch was on his way through the oldest part of the Naval Barracks at Chatham, known as Cumberland Block. His destination was Room No. 34, where the next man on the duty roster was still sleeping. The sentry was desperate for a break himself and meant to waken the oversleeping sentry, but before he reached Room No. 34, the sentry was set about by a crowd of prisoners who were intent of escaping. Without a second thought, the mob bludgeoned the sentry to death. During and since the 1940s several people have claimed to see and hear the sentry's ghost limping and tapping through old Cumberland Block.

A FIGHT AT FORT PITT

On August 10, 1830 John McAlister was indicted with assaulting William Rogers, a soldier at Chatham. McAlister stole from Rogers a watch and two sovereigns.

William Rogers was on his way home to his quarters at Fort Pitt about 10 p.m. McAlister and another soldier approached him, saying 'How d'y do, comrade?' and immediately knocked him down, kneeling on him as he lay helpless on the ground. McAlister then rifled the pockets of his victim, tearing his trousers as he removed the watch. Rogers yelled, 'Murder!' and the guard heard and came to his assistance. McAlister ran off but he was chased and captured with the stolen articles in his possession. He was found guilty but the paper made no mention of his punishment.

CRAZY WITH JEALOUSY

A sergeant, Patrick Feeney, had a fancy for a young private's pretty wife – at least, that's what the private believed. Crazy with jealousy, Private Benjamin Gardiner of the 50th Regiment, went looking for Sergeant Feeney and shot him dead. In July, 1834, Private Gardiner was hanged on Chatham Lines for the sergeant's murder. His execution was meant as a warning to his comrades, but during the proceedings, a storm blew up and it became very dark. People thought this was the wrath of God, and many of them ran away to hide from God's anger.

TRAGEDY AT BROMPTON BARRACKS

In August 1865, a soldier shot dead an officer on the parade ground at Brompton Barracks in Gillingham. The officer was Major Francis Horatio de Vere, a veteran of the Crimea, and his

Kitchener Barracks at Fort Amherst.

murderer was Sapper John Currie, who showed no remorse for his action towards his superior. It happened on 11 August, when the nineteen-year-old sapper fired just as the 400 men were standing to attention. Lieutenant Arthur Durnford rushed to help the fallen major, who was gasping 'Oh my God.' It was Lieutenant Durnford who later entered the barracks and discovered Currie alone in his cell, which reeked of gunpowder. Currie immediately and calmly admitted his guilt.

At first, it was feared that the wound to the major was fatal. Later, the surgeons felt that the victim would live but they were wrong and within a week. Major de Vere had died. At his trial at the Central Criminal Court, the unsavoury facts emerged. John Currie simply never got it right, while Major de Vere was among the most stringent officers of the Royal Engineers, demanding no less than the best from those under his command. The crunch came when Currie took a cut in pay for a misdemeanour which had taken place a few months previously. Currie's laziness continued, perhaps more out of grievance than for any other reason and he ended up in the guard house, then later his commanding officer had him shut in his cell for six days. John Currie decided he was being picked on, so he loaded up his rifle, and shot the major from the window over the heads of the assembled soldiers.

The defence claimed that John Currie, driven out of his mind by the alleged grievances, had been insane when he had committed the murder. However, the plea was rejected by the judge, Mr Justice Shee, who sentenced John Currie to death. Later it was claimed by a minister

The stone tablet commemorating Patrick Feeney's murder.

that John Currie had expressed remorse for killing the major and he was well-supported by his family and his prayers before his execution. Comforted by the Presbyterian minister, a Mr John Greener, John Currie asked for a prayer to be said as he was prepared for death. On the fateful day, as the hangman placed the noose around his neck, he waited for around five minutes for the duration of the prayer.

Once the drop fell, Currie took a couple of minutes to die, as was usual with those who suffered at the hands of dreaded William Calcraft.

THE DASHING DESERTER

According to the *Kentish Independent* dated Saturday 13 January 1900, a young sapper of the Royal Engineers deserted from the corps at Chatham. He tried to enlist in a regiment of Hussars intending to go to war, but his military appearance alerted the authorities, especially when his account of himself seemed so evasive. Immediately, he was placed under arrest, pending a court martial at Chatham on the following Thursday. However, while being escorted across the parade ground on the Wednesday afternoon, he managed to escape, taking the corporal in charge by surprise. So the dashing deserter got clean away!

16

THE WARSHIP MURDERER

The following murder, which happened in 1935, was extremely brutal and bloody, and yet it produced a dramatic aftermath where the felon suddenly became the victim and the centre of an intense rescue campaign masterminded by a wealthy widow.

IN COLD BLOOD

This murder took place on board the gunnery training ship, HMS *Marshal Soult*, Chatham. Leonard Albert Brigstock, a ship's stoker, who joined the Navy at seventeen years old, was consumed with a passion for the macabre which manifested itself in horrible, blood-filled dreams. Brigstock was thirty-three years old when he brutally slit the throat of Chief Petty Officer Hubert Sidney Deggan, aged thirty-six, on Saturday 19 January 1935. Most sinister of all, he attacked the officer while he was sleeping on the ship, which was then berthed in Chatham Dockyard.

Previously, Brigstock had been to the King William for pints and darts, leaving at 2.15 to return to his Nelson Road home. Then, although he was on leave, he decided to return to the ship, where he waited till Deggan had gone for a nap in the mess room. The vicious attack resulted in the head of the CPO becoming almost severed from the body. Coolly, Brigstock, soaked in blood, went to a shipmate to report what he'd done. 'I have cut the CPO's throat,' he told him, handing him the dripping razor.   It later emerged, after Brigstock was searched, that his motive was revenge for having been reported for three disciplinary offences by the murdered man. Apart from these issues, he had, apparently, a good record and was described as 'conscientious.' The offences involved negligence, such as absence and drinking tea at the wrong time and place and said to be of a very serious nature.

MITIGATING CIRCUMSTANCES?

Brigstock had experienced a traumatic life, suffering as he did from the death of his first wife and insanity, which appeared to have run in the family as his grandfather died in a lunatic asylum and his niece was in a mental home. His childhood was disturbed by his father's violent attacks on the family. However, Brigstock, too, was often violent and once tried to cut his brother's wrist with a knife. Some of Brigstock's dreams involved his dead wife. He saw her on the side of the ship trying to get away from an enormous figure – this was the Devil's mate. When he tried to save her, he was choked and beaten by the evil, black figure.

BRIGSTOCK'S WEALTHY CHAMPION

At the Kent Assizes a month later, Brigstock denied malicious and wilful murder, pleading insanity. His plea was rejected and the jury, after being out for fifteen minutes, found the ship's stoker guilty. Putting on his black cap, the judge pronounced the death sentence on Brigstock, who appealed but without success. His last hope was a reprieve which never happened. Leonard Brigstock was tried at Maidstone on 19 February 1935, by Judge Lord Chief Justice Lord Hewart and sentenced to hang on Tuesday 2 April, 1935 at Wandsworth.

On the day of the execution at Wandsworth, there was almost a riot outside the prison, for Leonard Brigstock's case had been taken up by the widow of a Belgian shaving-cream magnate. Mrs Violet Van der Elst waged an anti-capital punishment campaign from her Kensington home, having organised a petition totalling 65,000 signatures in favour of a reprieve. She maintained Brigstock was insane, therefore, he should not hang. Mrs Van der Elst was not successful in her campaign and Brigstock was duly executed despite her protests that they were hanging an innocent man. It appears there was a fairground atmosphere on the day of execution. Planes zoomed overhead trailing banners STOP THE DEATH SENTENCE while women prayed and men trundled around with sandwich boards saying: STOP CAPITAL PUNISHMENT. Excited crowds milled outside the prison gates reading leaflets against capital punishment. Someone shouted, 'England is about to commit another murder in cold blood.'

The hangman was Robert Baxter, assisted by Robert Wilson, who ensured that the trap dropped beneath Leonard Brigstock at 9 a.m. that April morning. His death was reported as being 'instantaneous'.

HANGMAN (OR HANGWOMAN) URGENTLY WANTED

After the notorious and brutal hangman William Calcraft retired, the position of hangman was no longer a salaried position and fees remained low throughout the period beginning around 1870 to the 1960s, when finally hanging was abolished. Human nature being what it is, in spite of the low fees, there was no shortage of applicants for the post of executioner and these included a number of women. Ghoulish? It certainly seems so.

17

TWO TRAGIC MOTHERS

It's always sad to hear of the murder of a young mother, not just for her own sake and for a young life cut short, but because of the effect of her loss upon her orphaned children. In the first of these two cases there seems to be little or no motive, since the young victim was a complete stranger to her attacker, while the second horrific murder was the result of a violent row between the young couple.

KEEP ON SMILING

Ellen Ann Symes, a thirty-four-year-old mother, was murdered by soldier, Gunner Reginald Sidney Buckfield on Friday 9 October 1942 near Brompton Farm Road, Strood. Ellen was married to Alfred James Symes, a joiner and at the time of her death, was around five months pregnant. The couple already had a four-year-old son.

Because Alfred worked on the night shift in a munitions factory, Ellen liked to visit her parents on a Friday night for company. They lived in Dickens Terrace, in Wainscott. After her visit, she put her small son Robin in his pushchair and her parents accompanied her part of the way home, leaving her at Wainscott Working Men's Club, so that by the time she got to Hollywood Road (now Hollywood Lane) at around 9.40 p.m. she was alone. Here, less than a quarter-of-a-mile from her home, she was brutally attacked as a man leapt on her, thrusting a knife into her throat. Staggering, the pushchair still in front of her, she fell into a gateway.

Mr Pattenden of a nearby property, *Valhalla,* heard a scream and a loud thud against the fence at the front of the house. He went to investigate and found it was a woman's body, bleeding on the ground, with a pushchair overturned beside it. The child was naturally scared but was unhurt. Later, the police found a knife with a yellow handle lying around 100yds from the site of the murder.

Dr Charles Greene arrived in due course, but Ellen's life had already ebbed away due to stab wounds in her neck. It was thought she had been attacked around 30yds back up the road. Naturally, this vicious and apparently motiveless attack terrified the women of Medway, who made sure all their windows and doors were secure and stayed indoors after dark.

The following day, the little boy was able to tell police that their attacker was a man in soldier's uniform. In due course, they interrogated Reginald Buckland, who'd gone missing on 26 September from his station at 542 Heavy Anti Aircraft Battery at Oak Street Camp. He'd enlisted in June 1940, and had originally come from Houghton near Mansfield where he had a wife and three children. He claimed that he'd deserted because he feared he might be found out for having an affair with an ATS girl. Already, he had a reputation as an undesirable character and had previously been questioned about two other murders, one in London and one in Southport although he was cleared in both cases. After his desertion, Buckland, who called himself 'Smiler', supported himself by fruit-picking.

The Steam Packet, Strood.

On the night of the murder he'd visited his regular pub, the Steam Engine, now known as the Steam Packet. He left just after 8 p.m. and went along to the Ship Inn at Frindsbury where he had a beer and a pie. Leaving just before nine, he walked through the streets until he came to Dillywood Lane. It was here six ATS girls got off a bus and Buckland followed them along Dillywood Lane, eventually lying down and sleeping by some haystacks before being arrested. Buckland was shown the murder weapon, a bone-handled knife, but he denied all knowledge of it and the police satisfied themselves that he was not guilty of murder, handing the absentee back to the military authorities.

Meantime, throughout Buckland's arrest and subsequent release, the search for the murderer intensified, involving questioning hundreds of soldiers and checking out uniforms for bloodstains. But Buckland himself was about to give the police a hand in finalising the investigation. He'd written a couple of short stories during the three days he was confined to his cell and together they comprised thirteen pages of text, with confusingly similar titles: *The Mystery of Brompton Road* and *The Mystery of the Brompton Road Murder*.

Buckland handed these stories to the detective in charge of him, probably out of pride or vanity, thus signing his death warrant. (Later, he was to claim the road referred to in the story was London's Brompton Road, not Medway's.) Buckland's writing was incoherent and confusing, but it conveyed detailed information about the movements of Mrs Symes that the author could not have known unless he had committed the murder. He helped the detectives further by freely admitting he hadn't read any of the newspaper reports about the murder. If this wasn't enough, the police hadn't told him anything at all about the murdered woman or the circumstances around her death.

On 7 November, Reginald Buckfield was removed from military custody to be charged with murder. Buckland's trial took place at the Old Bailey from Wednesday 20 January 1943. The trial focussed on the stories he had written – all other evidence to do with the case was purely circumstantial. Mr L.A. Byrne was the prosecutor and he put it to the court that the long narrative he had written while detained in custody could not have been produced without intimate knowledge of the death of the murdered woman. Then copies of the stories were circulated among the jury and the judge, Mr Justice Hallet and the clerk of the court, read them out over the next one-and-a-half hours. The first story had a character called Smiler who was a true Bluebeard, and was set in a pub, while the second story involved a murdered ATS girl. Buckfield's assertion to his counsel Hector Hughes that he wrote the stories because he was bored alone in his cell did not help. When asked, 'Why did you choose the name Brompton Road for the title?' Buckland tried to convince the court that it was just coincidence.

Within one hour of retiring, the jury found Buckland guilty. As Mr Justice Hallett passed sentence of death on Buckland, mentioning that this was a singularly cruel crime, the cold-blooded murderer smiled. It appears, however, that a medical enquiry was instigated by the Home Secretary, Mr Herbert Morrison, which certified him and, in March, the death sentence was reduced to life in Broadmoor, the criminal lunatic asylum. Buckland, the Smiler, is reported to have carried on smiling.

A TRAGEDY IN OLD BROMPTON

Harry Frampton, a young naval officer's steward at Royal Navy Barracks, Chatham, lived in River Street, Old Brompton in 1928 with his nineteen-year-old wife, Pat. Harry was just twenty-three and completely at a loss when faced with Pat's terrible temper. The fact she had her baby in her arms did not prevent her from lashing out at her husband one morning in April as they walked to the local railway station. Screaming abuse, she hit him again and again, but by now Harry had had enough. He had a razor hidden in his pocket and without warning, he slashed at Pat's neck. Still clinging to her baby, the deep wound gushing with blood, his wife didn't stand a chance and died just after reaching hospital. Meanwhile, Harry Frampton had disappeared.

It did not take the police long to locate Harry at his parents' house in Twickenham and on being questioned, he insisted the razor was not meant to harm his wife, only to frighten her. At this stage he was unaware the wound had been fatal, but soon the two policemen D.C. Hawes and D.I. Humphries informed the young steward he would be charged with his wife's murder. He was remanded in custody for one week before being charged with the wilful murder of his wife, Pat, whose real name was Maude Frampton.

On 27 June 1928 he appeared at Kent Assizes where more details of the young couple's life emerged. Frampton claimed he earned £1 4s a week and gave his wife £1 of that, but she wanted more. Desperately, Harry insisted that Pat should live at her brother's house in Twickenham to save money, but Pat was unwilling at first. Later she agreed but, as they left for the station, she'd flown into a rage and started kicking and hitting Harry. After a violent scene on the street, Harry got out the razor, later claiming that he hoped this would frighten her into silence. It only made her more furious. Then, Harry Frampton claimed, Pat grabbed the razor, pulling it towards herself.

The jury found Harry Frampton guilty within five minutes, although they recommended mercy, but Harry was sentenced to death. Subsequently, an appeal was unsuccessful, then the Home Secretary, Sir William Joynson-Hicks took the decision to commute the sentence to life imprisonment. (William Joynson-Hicks' constituency was Twickenham, Harry Frampton's home town.)

TRUE OR FALSE

Sometimes, felons are so desperate to avoid facing punishment for their crimes, they will say anything, however outrageous, to avoid conviction. Even so, it is difficult to see how Walter Smith could believe he could get away with such an out-and-out falsehood.

BLOODY MURDER ON A BARGE

Albert Baker, aged twenty-eight, was the skipper of a barge called the *East Anglia* which was owned by the London & Rochester Trading Co. Walter 'Ginger' Smith, a little older at thirty-three, was his mate and they were old friends, having shared a school and similar childhood in Strood. Their first trip as barge-mates was in October 1937, but tragically, this voyage was not to be repeated. Their friendship seemed to be a case of 'opposites attract', Albert being a cheerful soul and Walter Smith rather reticent and often depressed.

Albert had been separated from his wife and was staying with his mother, father and married sister in Gordon Road. He was from a river-going family and had even been in a film, *Captain Bull*, which was made in the Medway area.

Albert played the leader of a gang of smugglers and was actually offered further work, but he preferred to be a waterman. In general, he was a pleasant, well-balanced young man. Things were very different for Walter Smith. With an alcoholic father, a mother who suffered from epilepsy, and an aunt who'd met her death in a lunatic asylum, Walter had nothing like Albert's background advantages. Despite these differences, or maybe because of them, the two young men were said to behave like brothers.

On Thursday, 21 October, the *East Anglia* docked at Felixstowe with a cargo of barley. Albert and Walter were seen drinking together on the quayside Pier Hotel the following day, around noon. Then the two men returned to the barge. The following day, dockhands made a shocking discovery. Baker lay dead in his cabin on his bank, having been shot once in the left temple and twice in the chest, presumably by the long-barrelled pistol lying nearby. It seemed he'd also been robbed because his empty wallet was found beneath his pillow.

A LIKELY STORY!

That evening, at the British Lion pub, Smith was found drinking by the police who informed him his good friend was dead. He made no response except to request to be allowed to finish his drink, then he was taken to the police station, where he made his first fatal mistake. 'You say he was shot dead?' he enquired, artlessly. But the police had not told him how Albert had died. That evening, Walter Smith said he'd last seen Albert alive the evening before and he'd been arguing with a woman. She was Albert girlfriend and her name was Scottie. However, Scottie was not

Always a familiar sight on the Medway – barges today near Sun Pier.

These old barges have come to grief at Sun Pier, Chatham.

the best person for Smith to try to implicate if he wanted to shift suspicion from himself. Scottie was able to prove she'd been in London the whole weekend.

On Sunday, Smith's situation deteriorated even further. He told the police that he and Albert were drinking in the pub on Friday, but on returning to the barge, the two of them had argued and Albert pulled a gun on him. They struggled and the gun went off. The big question here is how a gun could 'accidentally' go off three times! Especially as that sort of gun had to be reloaded for each shot! Walter Smith was digging himself a pit and he was digging himself in deeper and deeper. Even stranger, he had worn the dead man's suit the previous Friday evening while treating all the pub's customers to drinks. Did the money come from the empty wallet under Albert's pillow?

The trial took three days and was held at Ipswich Assizes. His defending counsel, Mr Boileau did not attempt to dispute the fact Smith had fired the lethal shots, but claimed his client suffered from alcoholic insanity. Smith denied that he could recall firing the shots and his sister, Beatrix Rix, confirmed that after her brother had had a drink, he didn't know what he was doing.

STRANGER AND STRANGER

Police Inspector Bevan from Maidstone described a previous incident involving Walter Smith. In a drunken state, the accused had entered his police station around seven years previously. He'd presented the police with a carving knife claiming he'd just stabbed a man in the back. He was found to be lying and the only charge against him was for the theft of the knife. The policeman had been summoned by the defence to help prove that Walter Smith was unstable. Next, in came the expert, a Dr Cannon of Uxbridge, who co-managed mental homes. He claimed he did not find Smith insane, but of sub-normal mentality and that the excess of alcohol imbibed by the prisoner contributed to his condition. Thus, he had 'alcoholic insanity.' Another doctor was called who labelled Smith's condition as 'acute alcoholism'.

The prosecution disputed all of this, for their doctor, from Norwich Prison, said he could find no evidence of insanity. A Dr Grierson, from Brixton Prison, put forward his opinion, that Smith's long, wild periods of intense fury could make him commit violence but retain no memory of it. However, the judge had a very pertinent point to make, that going through the motions of loading and unloading a pistol hardly constituted a period of wild frenzy. Dr Grierson agreed and so Walter Smith's fate was sealed. It took the jury forty minutes to pronounce Walter Smith guilty. It is recorded that Walter Smith flinched but stayed calm.

'I MUST HAVE GONE OFF MY HEAD!'

There was an appeal but this was dismissed and on 8 March, Walter Smith was hanged at Norwich Prison. Before he died, Smith still insisted that he'd committed that terrible crime in a wild rage without knowing he'd done it – but the fact remained, how could you load a pistol three times while in a wild and drunken frenzy?

19

ONLY SHOWING OFF

ONLY SHOWING OFF

Thirty-three year-old PC Alan George Baxter was murdered by his namesake, twenty-year-old Alan Derek Poole in June 1951 for no good reason except Alan Poole fancied himself an anti-hero.

Alan Poole had been known as a 'bad lot' with a long history of offending. The first recorded offence was in 1946 for office-breaking, after which he was sent to an approved school. After absconding, he broke into a Chatham sports pavilion which resulted in three years' Borstal training. Again, Poole escaped but was arrested and sent back to Borstal.

This disturbed young man, who was one of ten children, was, by now, harbouring a pathological hatred of the police. But he adored American gangster films and comics and liked to model himself on their anti-heroes, talking like them, even honing his walk into a swagger just like a film-star gangster. He was equally thrilled by knives and weapons.

In 1949 Poole absconded once more but this time he threatened a constable with a knife and was sent back to Borstal yet again.

Then, on 5 June 1951, a young man, David Tutt and three male friends were confronted in the Luton area of Chatham by Alan Poole with two girls. Poole was masked and carried a Sten gun in the crook of his arm. Poole threatened the young men and they fled, but decided to tell the occupant of a nearby cottage about the hostile gunman. The cottager called his dog and returned to 'have a word' with the masked man but Poole merely fired another volley of rounds at them.

A 999 call was made to the police. PC Baxter, who lived in Palmerston Road, received the report of a gunman hiding in Luton, an area of Chatham. PC Baxter was an experienced officer, having been in the force since 1938. This unfortunate policeman was under some stress himself, as his father had recently died and his wife had given birth to a stillborn baby.

PC Baxter, who was based at the old police station just off New Road, went to investigate with two other PCs, Langford and Brown. At the Hen & Chickens in Luton Road, the policemen were waved down by the little group that had been fired on and they explained what had happened and where they thought the gunman was hiding. PCs Langford and Brown entered the corporation rubbish dump, while PC Baxter remained in the car. There were some huts surrounding the dump and PC Langford peered in the broken window of one of the huts and saw Poole and the two women opening the door. PC Langford rushed around to the front but was greeted by a hail of bullets from the automatic weapon. Fortunately, the shots missed and Langford escaped death by inches.

Meanwhile, Alan Poole ran to the police car and fired at it, shattering the windscreen. Drawing out his truncheon (Baxter was otherwise unarmed) the policeman pushed open the squad car door. But the gunman fired again and PC Alan Baxter was shot several times and fell to the ground, while Poole jumped over a gate and vanished.

Criminals had plenty of hiding places in Medway's dark and narrow alleys.

PC Langford tried to console PC Alan Baxter, but the latter seemed to know he could not survive his terrible wounds. 'I've had it. I'm going,' said the brave PC as he was rushed to St Bartholomew's Hospital.

A search ensued between Luton, Blue Bell Hill and Wigmore areas. Poole's two young women companions were found and turned out to be escapees from a Gloucester remand home. They explained that Poole had stolen the Sten gun when he was a member of the Royal Corps of Signals. They also said that Alan Poole was only 'showing off' when he attacked PC Langford on the Monday night.

Poole's parents lived at No. 114 Symons Avenue, where armed police surrounded the house, believing the perpetrator of this awful crime to be inside. At 8 a.m., Alan Poole's father Albert returned from his night shift and everything was silent till next morning when eleven-year-old sister, Doreen, left to go to school. Unexpectedly, she returned home, very upset. The other girls had laughed at her because they'd heard her brother, Alan, had shot at a policeman. Mrs Poole sat down to write a note to the school, but Alan, overhearing, told his family to get out, as he was going to 'shoot it out with the cops.' He was talking wildly, and was still under the influence of the American media, 'They'll never take me alive. I'll kill the bastards.'

At 9 a.m. Mrs Poole and her daughter left the house and there was a burst of Sten gun fire from the back. Alan Poole had moved about 50yds away from the house and opened fire in the direction of his father. The armed police closed in as Poole retreated to an upstairs bedroom continuing to fire, indiscriminately, at police. Reinforcements were called for and some people said it was exactly like a siege.

The police decided to introduce tear gas grenades, but still Alan Poole carried on with his furious bombardment. Eventually, a group of police officers led by Chief Supt, C.F. Broughton bashed down the door and rushed inside. Soon, there was a white handkerchief waving out of a window to tell everyone outside that it was over. Poole had been killed by the last round of return fire. PC Baxter died in hospital eighteen hours after admittance and was laid to rest on the 11 June. The following day, 12 June, the funeral was held of Alan Poole, his cold-hearted murderer.

20

IMMORALITY AND PROSTITUTION

The following are cases of immorality and prostitution, widely ranging in severity and reported according to the morality and beliefs of their time. We may be either shocked or amused at the way our predecessors viewed their world - but imagine if they had the same advantages that we do and could pass judgement on our world today? How would we fare, I wonder?

THIEVES AND VAGABONDS

The village of Upchurch lies on the outskirts of Rainham. This is an entry from the journal of the Vicar of Upchurch, John Woodruff, dated 24 April 1851.

> April 24 – Walked to Hartlip hill to attend a police meeting, being one of the inspectors for Upchurch; there are three men employed who live respectively at Newington, Hartlip Hill and Rainham. Yesterday, being Upchurch fair brought into the Parish a number of itinerant beings. My dogs (one indoors) barked violently about two o'clock this morning. I have just learned from the Policeman that he was round my house ... and that he cleared the Village of the tramps immediately after the fair. What a great pity it is that such fairs cannot be suppressed. They only cause a great deal of immorality to be committed, bring a number of pilfering gipsies into the neighbourhood and benefit no one but the Publican who lives upon the drunkenness of others.

(It is believed that Edmund Drake, the Vicar of St Mary's Church in Upchurch in 1560, was Sir Francis Drake's father. Originally from Dover, Edmund moved to Medway to become naval chaplain at Chatham Dockyard.)

THOROUGHLY SHAMEFUL CONDUCT

A disgraceful exhibition of bad taste took place at Gillingham Fair in 1868. The Revd J. Leach, Vicar of Gillingham, declared the mart was no longer held for its proper purpose but had degenerated to 'nothing but noise, riot and confusion.' It seemed there were too many men from the barracks and women of 'low order' for the sensitive vicar. On Gillingham Green, on Sabbath evenings, half-naked men fought in a ring, cheered on by obscene language from their supporters.

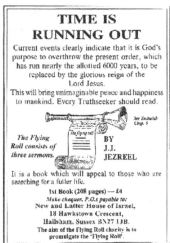

TIME IS RUNNING OUT

Current events clearly indicate that it is God's purpose to overthrow the present order, which has run nearly the allotted 6000 years, to be replaced by the glorious reign of the Lord Jesus.

This will bring unimaginable peace and happiness to mankind. Every Truthseeker should read.

See Zechariah
Chap. 5

The Flying Roll consists of three sermons.

BY
J.J.
JEZREEL

It is a book which will appeal to those who are searching for a fuller life.

1st Book (208 pages) — £4
Make cheques, P.O.s payable to:
New and Latter House of Israel,
18 Hawkstown Crescent,
Hailsham, Sussex BN27 1JB.
The aim of the Flying Roll charity is to promulgate the 'Flying Roll'.

DRUNK IN CHARGE OF THE NEW AND LATTER DAY HOUSE OF ISRAEL

James Jershom Jezreel (born in 1851, real name James Roland White) enlisted in the British army on 27 July 1875, and joined the sixteenth Regiment of Foot in Chatham, Kent. He became interested in a religious sect known as the *Jezreelites* in England. The sect was founded by Joanna Southcott who believed she would mother the new Messiah – at sixty-five years old – but she died in 1814, childless. James Jezreel was convinced he was the 'Messenger of the Lord' and was responsible, in 1881, for the erection of Jezreels Tower in Gillingham. The Tower stood 120ft high on the site of the present-day Jezreel's bus stop until it was demolished in 1961. At that time a sealed bottle was discovered under a foundation stone containing details of the sect. Jezreel is a real place found in the *Book of Revelations* and refers to Armageddon and the battle between good and evil.

This is why it has found its way into this chapter on immorality, because its founder, James Jezreel, who insisted his followers abstain from drink, was constantly drunk and falling about the place. Although that's not exactly a serious crime, it's unseemly behaviour for the leader of a religious sect who is supposed to set an example to his flock. Eventually, James Jezreel became a very heavy drinker, and he became ill and died on 2 March 1885.

A SHOCKING SIGHT FOR INNOCENT TRAVELLERS

On 30 April 1870 according to the *Chatham News*, a case was heard at Rochester involving three boys named Letley, Park and Ring. The boys were charged with unlawfully bathing in the mill pond in Canal Road, Strood, on 15 April. This was contrary to the byelaws and caused great annoyance to public good taste. The mill pond backed onto Doggetts Square, where Parks and Letley apparently ran naked, by the railway on the other side of the pond.

Mr Price, the stationmaster, explained how the pond was a very short distance from the north Kent railway station and the boys' constant bathing was a source of great annoyance to the passengers travelling to and from the station. The court told Mr Price he should give his employees instructions to watch out for the naked boys and especially, to try to catch any 'larger boys' who committed this offence. Letley and Parks were ordered to attend court again in one

Opposite left: Jezreels Tower, located on the site of the present-day Jezreels bus stop.

Opposite right: A flyer for the New and Latter House of Israel

Right: Canal road sign.

Railway arches close to Watermill Stairs, Canal Road – now a dumping ground for discarded shopping trolleys.

month's time, but meantime should inform all their companions that they would be severely punished if they re-offended by bathing in the mill-pond outside of the prescribed hours (before 7 a.m. or after 9 p.m.).

The paper printed a short piece on Saturday 23 July to report that the boys were discharged so presumably they did not repeat the offences, or, if they did, they weren't caught.

UNEQUAL OPPORTUNITIES

In Victorian times, there was a vigorous upsurge in prostitution, in particular from Star Hill in Rochester to Sun Pier in Chatham. Trade around the River Medway area and its dockyard meant there were always many young men, soldiers and sailors, as well as military and engineering workers, some of them far from home. All of them were looking for sex and excitement. Not much better was the area around Corporation Street, formerly known as the Common, where animals were kept on their way to market. Like the Brook, these areas were slums, steeped as they were in poverty and those employed on river work. At the height of its bawdiness during

Left: Rochester Bridge.

Opposite left: The Tudor Rose pub.

Opposite right: Upnor village signpost.

the mid-1800s, Chatham was a riot of soldiers, sailors and prostitutes, high on booze and sex. The police, at this time, were inadequate to deal with the situation.

Pubs and brothels, seedy street bars and the backs of shops and alleyways all provided venues for every kind of 'adventure' and, apart from the regular prostitutes, there were plenty of poor working-class women eager, or desperate enough, to provide what these men wanted. The women had little choice, since there were few jobs available for them in an area dominated by the masculine pursuits of ship-building, engineering and other fields of work pertaining to Medway's military presence. They had to work or they would, quite simply, starve.

If anyone was arrested in the 1880s, it could set off a chain reaction. 'All it took to spark off a riot was for the police to arrest a drunk and take him up to New Road where the police station was, and they would be followed by a stone-throwing mob who would try to climb over the station walls.' (*The Chatham Scandal*, by Brian Joyce, 1999)

The Tudor Rose at Upnor was once a brothel, serving soldiers from nearby Upnor Castle. The castle was built around 1559 and the pub is almost as old and was formerly known as the King's Head. It's easy to imagine how pretty little Upnor Village became a den of vice during Tudor and Victorian times with its close proximity to the castle.

Eventually, the Government cracked down in an attempt to try to halt the spread of VD among servicemen. In 1869, the Contagious Diseases Act permitted the police to register working prostitutes and ensure they had regular medical examinations and those who tested positive were detained in hospital for nine months. Occasionally, things went wrong and malicious accusations were made so that one or two virgins found themselves being examined for contagious disease. (The police had even tried to get pub licences revoked to prevent the women from plying their trade on their premises. It is reported that in 1864, Supt Radley attempted to have seven pubs shut down, the Lord Nelson, the Bear and Staff, the Five Bells, the Flushing, the Homeward Bound, the Duke of Gloucester and the Maidstone Arms. The Magistrates disagreed, perhaps fearing a street riot, so everything continued as it was.)

There were nine brothels in Chatham and around three hundred prostitutes in 1870, but eleven years later, the number had halved to 150 due to the Government crackdown.

A 'REFUGE' FOR PROSTITUTES

Eliza Hook was a trial to her mother, Frances. Shortly before Christmas in 1889, she abandoned her position as a maid and ran away. Some time later, she resided near her family in Greenwich, to learn the laundry trade. What seems apparent is that during this time, she had sex with a man who had offered to marry her and she ended up in a refuge for prostitutes in Chatham. Mrs Hook denied that Eliza was a prostitute, although it seems unlikely that Eliza would have volunteered the information to her mother. Also, poverty made prostitutes of many unfortunate, lower-class women.

While she was at the Chatham House of Refuge, Eliza was visited by Frances only once and her mother claimed she thought her daughter seemed happy. The refuge, run by local clergy and businessmen, housed a variety of young women, including a few older girls who had formerly been making their way as prostitutes. It's claimed the girls and young women were kept virtual prisoners in this Chatham so-called refuge – in reality they could discharge themselves at any time, but they had nowhere else to go. They were made to attend church regularly and had to learn the laundry trade.

Poor Eliza paid dearly for her spirited unruliness – with her own death. But before she died, she put her mother right about the terrible treatment she'd received at the hands of the matrons. This is the series of crimes perpetrated against Eliza and probably other young women in the home:

- ❖ Given only dry bread to eat
- ❖ Shut up at weekends.
- ❖ Dipped in a cold water tub and made to work in a wet chemise.
- ❖ Held down in a tub for so long she thought she would drown.
- ❖ Threatened with beating if she complained to her mother or anyone else.
- ❖ Twelve hours a day standing in steaming heat, elbow deep in washing.
- ❖ Made to work barefoot.
- ❖ Beaten if she was too weak to do her work.
- ❖ Nicknamed 'the long lamp post' by the other girls because of her scragginess.

Generic view of the workhouse.

When the doctor eventually saw Eliza as she lay dying in the Chatham Workhouse Infirmary, he was shocked at her condition and the obvious neglect she'd been subjected to through starvation and torture. One of the most horrific manifestations of this appalling neglect was a dead bone which stuck out from one of her toes, giving off a terrible stench. She had ulcers on her ankle and a painful swelling on her hip. Her hair was rife with vermin and the doctor asserted he'd seldom seen a patient in such a terrible state. Eliza weighed only 5st by now, less than most eight-year-olds at that time.

The post-mortem reported death from pneumonia, although her poor health was exacerbated by neglect. Jane Davey, the matron, denied all the charges, explaining that none of the other girls complained. If a girl was disobedient, the usual punishment was simply being sent to her dormitory until she repented. Miss Davey swore that everything Eliza had said was a lie, although she admitted that she'd been lax in not sending for a doctor immediately. All the same, Eliza was always ready to fight with the other girls. Davey's assistant, Eliza Brown, also denied ducking and almost drowning her charge.

The jury decided the matrons had been careless, but this carelessness was not enough to embark on criminal proceedings. They were told they were not to let anything like this happen again. The people of Chatham were furious and mobbed the women's coach as they drove away from the court, throwing stones and rubbish at the windows. The Police had to protect the refuge staff from the crowds, even when they were back inside the refuge.

'SHOW ME THE WAY TO GO HOME'

Henry Thompson was a thirty-six-year-old Welsh coal miner who left his family, a wife and five children, in January 1926, but for good reason. He'd got himself a well-paid job at Chatham and had every intention of sending for his family once he'd sorted out his life. Rose Smith, who lived at No. 36 Cross Street, seemed a decent sort of landlady; she was forty-one and sociable, enjoying a drink and a chat with friends just like anyone else. At the time, her husband was serving in the Royal Navy.

Naturally, Henry was lonely and being in very close proximity to an attractive woman, he succumbed to temptation and the two became lovers. Henry was soon 'Uncle Harry' to Rose's children. The trouble was, Rose was more than generous with her favours and while Henry wanted her all to himself, she took other men into her bed. Mad with jealousy at this discovery, Henry confronted Rose and they quarrelled. On 8 February, 1926, Henry Thompson seized a razor, took hold of Rose and slit her throat.

Horrified at what he had done, Henry Thompson called the police and was tried by Judge Justice Herridge on 20 February 1926 at Maidstone Assizes. He was found guilty and sentenced to death. The famous Thomas Pierrepoint was appointed executioner, assisted by William Willis, and so the unfortunate prisoner, Henry Thompson, met his end on 9 March 1926. It is reported the Welshman remained calm throughout his time in the condemned cell and the day before the execution played cards with his warders whilst belting out a hearty rendition of *Show Me the Way to Go Home*.

WOMEN'S RIGHTS!

Looking at newspaper reports during the 1830s, one can imagine just how brave women had to be to stand up for their rights and how hard it was for poor women, especially prostitutes, in the prevailing attitudes of those times. Here's a poem which appeared in the *Rochester Gazette*, 6 April 1830.

The Fair Sex

When Eve brought woe to all mankind
Old Adam called her wo-man.
But when she woo'd with love so kind;
He then pronounced her woo-man;
But now with folly and with pride,
Their husbands' pockets trimming,
The ladies are so full of whim
That people call them whim-men.

And that, I am afraid, is actually one of the kinder, more reasonable poetical offerings of the time.

BIBLIOGRAPHY

Glover, Judith, *The Place Names of Kent* (1982) Meresborough Books

Greysmith, David, *Richard Dadd* (1973) Studio Vista

Hawkings, David T., *Criminal Ancestor* (1992) Alan Sutton Publishing Ltd

Lane, Brian, *The Murder Club* (1988) Harrap Ltd

MacDougall, Philip, *Murder in Kent* (1989) Robert Hale

Platt, Richard, *Smuggling in the British Isles, A History* Tempus Publishing Ltd www.smuggling.co.uk

Rayner, Stephen, 'The Tower of Mystery Surrenders its Secrets', Memories page, *Medway News*, May 2006 www.medwaymemories.co.uk

Schmalleger, Frank, *Criminology Today* (1999) Prentice Hall

Tomlinson, Norman, *The Book of Gillingham* (1979) Barracuda Books Ltd

www.stand-and-deliver.org.uk/highwaymen

AFTERWORD

'Murder is always a mistake – One should never do anything that one cannot talk about after dinner.'

Oscar Wilde (1854-1900) *The Picture of Dorian Grey*, chapter 19 (1891)

Above left: Spyhole, Upnor Castle.

Above right: Cannons at Upnor.

Right: River Medway, Upnor.

Other local titles published by Tempus

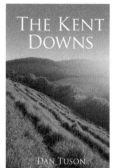

The Kent Downs
DAN TUSON

Nestled within the heart of the county, sparsely settled and largely untouched by the pressures of the modern age, the Kent Downs are home to some of the most enchanting countryside in southern England. This book unravels the history of the area's settlement and colonisation, the inspiration it has given to poets, artists and authors and the legacy of its rich and varied natural treasures. Richly illustrated with over 100 stunning photographs in colour and monochrome, the book will appeal to all those who visit, work or live in this cherished part of the county of Kent.

978 07524 4405 5

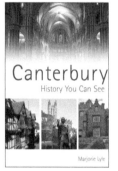

Canterbury History You Can See
MARJORIE LYLE

A day trip to Canterbury can feel like being 'punch-drunk'. Sometimes there is too much history to see. Great buildings like cathedrals can dwarf their neighbours and smother the memory of their various builders. City walls, seventeen centuries old, hide the changes which altered them; yet every building which has survived war, slump, plague and changing fashion has been adapted to new uses. Marjorie Lyle received a Civic Award from the City of Canterbury in 2005 for making the City's history available to a wider public by energetic and sustained research.

978 07524 4538 0

Who's Buried Where in Kent
ALAN MAJOR

This fascinating book will leave you humbled, uplifted and smiling. Within its pages the reader will discover the famous, infamous, notable, curious and eccentric people who were buried in Kent's churches, churchyards and cemeteries. Revised and updated, the book retains the A-Z format from the successful original volume published in 1990, now out of print. Sadly, even those people who were renowned in their lifetime are soon forgotten, their graves becoming overgrown and the inscriptions virtually illegible. Within the pages of this book Alan Major highlights the importance of recording these inscriptions and grave sites before they vanish forever.

978 07524 45441

Gravesham
JOHN GUY

Gravesham was the first town outside London that lent itself to the needs of society people seeking leisure. As it had the facilities of the coast but was situated only a few miles from the metropolis it acquired a number of elegant buildings that give the present-day town an air of grace and grandeur not normally found at such riverside towns. Illustrated with around 150 old photographs, prints and other printed ephemera, the book presents a complete historical picture of the region including a chapter on the outlying villages that make up the borough of Gravesham.

978 07524 4257 0

If you are interested in purchasing other books published by Tempus, or in case you have difficulty finding any Tempus books in your local bookshop, you can also place orders directly through our website

www.tempus-publishing.com